Mapping a New Reality

Discovering Intuitive Intelligence

Therese Rowley, Ph.D.

DEDICATION

I dedicate this book to my daughter, Ana Joy Pei, who is my daily touchstone to what is real, to what can emerge in love, and to the realization of joy's potential.

CONTENTS

FOREWORD

If ever I had a spiritual soul twin, Therese Rowley would be that woman. Both of us were born and raised in Chicago, where we both still reside. We both come from seriously Catholic backgrounds that did not leave us scarred but in fact led us deeply into the mystical depths of the Catholic tradition. And perhaps for that very reason, both of us became highly skilled intuitives who frame our work within an understanding of how the natural order of a conscious universe functions. The great Catholic mystics, particularly those who lived before the Age of Reason, were well familiar with the landscape of the conscious universe that we are now "re-discovering".

My favorite Catholic saint, Teresa of Avila, the first woman Doctor of the Catholic Church and a renowned Mystical Theologian, for example, wrote extensively about how the soul progresses through stages of consciousness. Such a process of maturation refines the inherent senses of the soul, one of which is our capacity to intuit guidance or receive instructions from spiritual guides or saints. Nothing that Therese Rowley has presented in this fine book, in other words, would surprise Teresa of Avila, who lived 500 years ago. Paradoxically, it will no doubt strike some if not many people as a bit challenging because in the five centuries between the time of Teresa of Avila and now, we have lost our innate capacity to resonate with all things extraordinary and have instead chosen to believe that reality is made of concrete and ruled by the ticking of a clock. For so many people, their self-esteem is measured by what they are paid per hour. During the time of Teresa of Avila, you would more likely be asked, "What exactly *is* an hour and how to you measure its value?" The idea that an hour could determine your worth as a human being would have been considered preposterous. And yet, has this society not collectively chosen to make that value and equation part of its reality?

Perhaps you are beginning to see in some small way that we human beings have always created or mapped our reality. We have always made up what we needed to believe at any given time, appropriate to supplies, circumstances, disasters, and population – not to mention politics and religion. Simultaneously, great masters and teachers have always come along to offer instruction into what has always been consistently the truth. For example, at present our society believes a particular bank of facts about various areas of research such as aspirin, molecules, space travel, and eating meat. Scientists eager to earn a reputation produce papers declaring their "scientific findings" as a new "truth" within days, if not hours, of the completion of their experiments. Usually within weeks, opposing scientific teams challenge that new "truth".

Genuine truth, however, is a constant, a given. It is law. Truth is, by its nature, a universal or cosmic construct that cannot be altered or challenged because it simply _IS._ The cosmic law: As Above, So Below is one such example of a cosmic truth. What is in One is in the Whole, is yet another. These laws are unbendable, irrefutable. They are simply Truth itself.

In, *Mapping a New Reality*, Therese has accomplished the formidable task of weaving cosmic truth together with subjective experiences. No scientists will emerge who can challenge the reality of cosmic truth because it simply *IS.* This was no small task. In fact, it was a masterful undertaking. I know as I have faced countless moments of wondering what words to use to describe the indescribable to audiences, such as when I am asked, "How do you do a medical intuitive reading? How does that work?" Imagine that what you experienced all your life and what you knew to be real and true was indeed a very real science, but not one that fit into our model of science. Yet, its capacity to heal, see beyond the boundaries of time and space, collect data, and advance the inner resources of humanity was immeasurable.

Therese has managed not only to illustrate the existence of this realm of energy science that has always existed, but she has provided examples of its components through her own work. Her professional readings, for example, may include accessing data from an individual's hidden personal history or perhaps a past life. Carefully weaving this data into present day circumstances, Therese manages to assist an individual in alleviating sufferings that ordinary counseling medical treatment is unable to do. She has earned a sterling reputation for her readings not just within her personal practice, but at the corporate level. Very few intuitives have been able to make it through the scrutiny of the "rational corporate key hole" and earn the respect of people whose focus is business survival. And yet, she brought and continues to bring to them a far more conscious perspective regarding the meaning and purpose of their choices in the world, which is, in a word, amazing.

And therein lies the true power of understanding this parallel reality of which she writes. This realm of energy data is real. It is the "dark matter" of our consciousness, of our very being. We are incomplete without including this knowledge into our understanding of human nature and human anatomy as well as our spiritual anatomy.

I also need to add that I think it takes enormous courage to relay this profound information in the form of an autobiography. Therese has revealed her own journey in this book, one I personally know to be authentic. She is a woman of impeccable integrity and deep spirituality. Her life has taken her through the darkest of dark nights and into the depths of authentic mystical experiences.

I deeply believe that this book in not only one that is essential for those who desire to understand the nature of the energy realm, it is necessary, as Therese does not hide her relationship to God. I'm not sure many people have the courage to openly speak about their love of Christ. Therese is a mystic who resides out of a monastery. She is a mother and has a corporate background. And, she still "takes her shoes off when walking on Sacred ground". To my mind, that makes her exceptional, bold, and brave. I am filled with admiration for how she has remained fully congruent to everything she believes in.

Caroline Myss

PREFACE

I have hemmed and hawed for thirty years or more, trying to translate my inner experience of Light to something useful and meaningful to those who have not shared the Light in this way. The path has finally revealed itself.

I considered standing with and behind ancient ways of Knowing. I thought about simply reinforcing meditation and prayer as the most important ways to Know and access what is well beyond logic's comprehension—methods whose pathways offer a quality of life that is unspeakably fulfilling. Indeed, these two practices are foundational to my way of Knowing and the methods I advocate in my work.

However, after facilitating large-scale transformation in business for over twenty-five years, and facilitating healing and individual transformation for thousands of diverse clients through intuitive Readings, I feel compelled to share the more textured ways of Knowing I have learned. As I connected the dots among the territories of fear, essential gifts, persistent challenges that are soul lessons, destiny points, and life purpose, an invisible map of reality began to emerge. Then my clients' stories taught me how the boundaries of their maps are significantly influenced and shaped by their ancestors, other lifetimes, and loved ones who have passed.

My passion and mission is to make the invisible visible; to move, as evidenced by my ChicagoNow.com blog, "From Paranormal to Pretty Normal." I want everyone to know how to identify and access their unique wisdom, and to begin to apply intuitive intelligence as clearly, readily, and as often as they do social and emotional intelligences.

I am compelled to build bridges upon which those with extra perceptions and those whose perceptions are more traditional and reasoned can meet and begin to better understand each other. In *Mapping a New Reality*, the bridges are made of metaphors and glued with logic to enhance a sense of safety in the journey. The principles used to companion those who want to make the passage are culled and adapted from both business and individual stories of transformation.

To those whose traditions are firm, I hope the bridges reveal that intuition is common among all humans, and that development and diverse intuitive expressions are universally available. I hope the bridges positively respond to evolution's mysterious transformational call to enhance our self-knowledge, accept more of our spiritual nature, and fulfill greater capacities in human expression.

This bridge building comes from a place deep inside me that insists I respect the perceptions on all sides of the connections I seek to make. Thus, I have worn many disguises over my spiritual self since I emerged from my large, Irish, storytelling family: from banker to corporate management consultant to independent change management consultant to skilled intuitive Reader, healer, and medium, to university adjunct professor, to speaker, to instructor of intuitive intelligence, and now author.

My understanding has been enriched by what I have witnessed in the inner and outer worlds of intuitive Reading clients who include business leaders and professionals, individuals on a spiritual path, parents of children with intuitive gifts, and the children themselves. Clients run the gamut of beliefs, from "just spiritual" to conservative Jews to fundamentalist Christians to Buddhists to Hindus to progressive Christians to atheists.

My diverse master's education covers both not-for-profit and business, and my other education and extensive explorations include body-centered psychotherapy and over fifty alternative healing modalities.

I have come to this conclusion: Life Is One Whole Story whose story lines can be traced to their source and named, whose tapestry can be seen and understood, and whose themes and threads can be un-twined into their original purpose.

I have also come to see the essential power of forgiveness to unravel all story lines and leave on the ground the motifs that can become fodder for the forest floor, upon whose foundation new stories may emerge.

While my intent in this book is to honor all perspectives, if your interpretation of life is far afield from mine, first trust yourself to know what best works for your learning and the richness of your life. If you find even a small desire to explore in more depth my unique translation of spirit into intuition, and then into boots-on-the-ground application, I hope you allow the challenge, cross the bridge, and find on the other side a gift that enhances your expression of Divine connection.

SO MANY THANKS

On the top of my gratitude list is the Divine company to which we all have access for the asking. To the God of my Heart, Christ; to His Blessed Mother; and to the saints and angels who have inspired my life, thank You for companioning me through this stunningly confusing journey so that I could find in the chaos some strings that, when tied together, may serve other souls.

I thank my dear father, Dr. Eugene Rowley, who passed in 2003—which was just yesterday in eternal time—for his gentleness, sensitivity, and kindness, which formed my sense of safety in the world and allowed this unique expression to emerge.

My mother, Jane Rowley, has taught me what it means to live a life devoted to Christ. Her kindness, wisdom, grace, lifelong companionship, and prayerful support have been my rock and compass.

I thank my ten siblings: Bobbie, Gene, Ed, Mary, John, Tom, Ann, Paul, Laura, and Dan, and their spouses, as well as my twenty-five nieces and nephews, for their gifts of humor, generosity, and community.

I thank Jen Weigel, the angel and friend whose generous arms reached out and jettisoned me into the public eye and brought so many to my door, whom I since then have had the privilege to serve.

I thank Ann Rowley Gilbert, Jane Cahill, Sue Manganiello, Linda Carter, Annie Marquez, Randi Fiat, Suzanne Lovell, Mary Wachowski,

Tina Guziec, Amy O'Keeffe, Carole Dunbar, Colleen Frasure, David and Leo Rosen, Bliss Browne, Caroline Myss, Jason Seiden, Tom Hall, and Elizabeth Londo for their friendship, inspiration and support in both bleak and joyous times.

This book went through a lifetime of integration and nine years of development, including the generous editing support of Tina Guziec, Randi Fiat, Mary Moye-Rowley, Jen Weigel and developmental editor Annie Andrews, who finally influenced me to use my own voice in memoir format. Bernadette Elenteny Joyce was my talented, professional and patient graphic and interior designer.

May you find in these pages what lifts your soul to its highest and most joyful expression.

INTRODUCTION

Inside each of us lives an invisible force that informs and shapes our lives. It is comprised of a kaleidoscope of belief systems, experiences, hopes and fears, family patterns, archetypes, and what has been passed down from ancestral lines. These elements move through silent inner pathways, making them difficult to access and understand. Yet they have power to overshadow all the carefully constructed outward order over which we think we have control.

When these hidden elements are made visible and are *meaningfully connected*, the opportunity arises for more positive, life-changing choices. Understanding your unique blueprint can prompt self-compassion, causing you to change the way you make sense of painful experiences. These blueprints connect to your life's purpose, and they allow you to access the lessons your soul came to this planet to learn. They help you understand why persistent challenges can be life-giving and why what you most desire can be so elusive.

Inside this hidden territory are forces that drive you to desire one path over another. They compel you to engage in relationships that initially attract but may later repel or confuse you. They urge you to perceive a situation in a way that is notably different from others' interpretation, and they move your heart to choose what has particular meaning, even when your choice may seem unfathomable to those closest to you.

For thirty years, I have been bridging visible and invisible worlds for those who are seeking to more fully understand relationships or situations in their lives that have become challenging—whether personally, within families, or in businesses. As a sacred witness, I enter into the process of energetically leaving this known and trusted world to cross the threshold into unfamiliar landscapes—landscapes that reveal stories, unconscious aspects, and metaphors that connect to the deeper meaning behind a person's hardships and life lessons.

As a business consultant and skilled intuitive who sees the world in wholes and systems, I have come to view this force as an invisible map, a map that makes up the perception of reality each of us uniquely holds, and through which we come to understand ourselves, others, and the world in which we live.

While some feel that their inner life is a jumble of unconscious musings that stumble into dreams and intrude intermittently in their lives, I have found that the invisible map of reality has organizing principles that help us understand dilemmas from a higher-order perspective. Values-laden boundaries hold together how we perceive and define reality at the moment, until new events and experiences expand understanding and broaden the map.

Maps are also influenced by the outward environment we daily encounter. Within each of the confines of our favorite venues, there exists a particular "Collective Force" comprised of thoughts, emotions, and strong beliefs. Without awareness, this force sways us, subtly insinuating its way into our behavior. Despite the authority of the Collective Force, there is a way we can stay in our power and assure that our map's boundaries are consciously secure.

Within the category of Collective Force, there are three primary influences. The first is what some call "past lives" and others call "archetypes" whose magnetic qualities act upon us like a full moon on the tides. The second is ancestral patterns that hand down pathways of habit and hope from which we can continue learning. One final influence is the imprint left upon us when the veil between worlds lifts, and then drops, as our loved ones pass to the Other Side. As I have leaned into the Light to perceive the worlds of those who are full of joy in Oneness, as well as those who live between humanity and the Light, I have Heard their stories and witnessed how they can overshadow a well-planned life, bringing more grace or greater challenge.

The invisible map of reality we each hold has specific territories worth exploring. The landscape includes life purpose, essential gifts, soul lessons disguised as persistent challenges, destiny points, and fear-based beliefs. When we understand this landscape as a family of related geographies, we have the opportunity to become familiar with these lands and align them with outer objectives, enhancing the power of our intention.

How do we access our inner map to make alignment possible? Toward this end, it is essential to befriend our intuition as an intelligence. Rather than hoping for a "hit" of gut wisdom or sudden revelation, we can access and develop the bridge between everyday reality and our inner map, making truth and wisdom ongoing companions in life's journey.

Through an exploration of my own evolution from Catholic mystic to business professional to teacher of intuitive intelligence, and through many intriguing stories of both intuitive Reading clients and business consulting clients, *Mapping a New Reality* offers you the opportunity to investigate your own hidden realms and make new sense of your life.

It is my hope that as you read this book, you will begin to see some unexpected interconnectedness within and among the stories in your life that enhance their meaning. As you learn about the elements of the invisible map of reality, I hope you will use the new insight—or reminder—to shape a future that supports the self you were meant to express.

This three-part book offers you the opportunity to:

• understand the evolution of my worldview

• learn the elements and interconnectedness among the territories in and around our invisible map of reality, and how these can lead us to our truth and wisdom; and

• discover why establishing intuition as an intelligence benefits you, your children, your business, and our world.

Part I is a memoir that moves through childhood and teenage mystic experiences to events that influenced a translation from spirit and energy to intuition. This translation resulted in working with clients to facilitate healing by "Reading" the intimate details of clients' invisible map of reality and helping them align with their purpose and gifts. Stories illustrate the unlikely marriage of these hidden and visible worlds.

Part II offers intuitive Reading client stories that illuminate the territories that comprise the invisible map of reality we each uniquely hold. These territories include inner influences of life purpose, essential gifts, soul lessons disguised as persistent challenges, and destiny points. Outer influences that shape our maps include other lives/archetypes, ancestral patterns, and loved ones who have passed. Stories also illuminate the qualities that are most essential to accessing the truth and wisdom within our invisible maps.

Part III provides perspectives about intuitive intelligence as the bridge between the sometimes-painful symptoms of everyday life and access to the truth that can realign us on our path. This Part includes an exploration of the phenomenon of an increasing number of children with high intuitive giftedness and how they are often misdiagnosed as "learning disordered." Examples of intuitive Readings with children offer intriguing possibilities for moving from masking and medicating symptoms for the sake of social survival to offering a lens of giftedness and positive development so children can contribute their gifts, which may help us resolve shared global challenges.

Note: Where capital letters are used related to the five senses and heart, "Seeing," "Hearing," "Knowing," etc, it indicates that the author is receiving information through her intuition.

Part I: *Memoir: From Wholeness to Fragmentation*

My worldview was founded upon many intimate spiritual experiences in childhood. It developed through confusing times when I could no longer access familiar Divine guidance. My attempts to grasp for sacred meaning, even in dark times, resulted in a unique translation of lessons learned in my early mystic years to later personal and business realities.

CHAPTER ONE

An Invitation from the Mystery of Life

My brother Tom once informed me, "Therese, your common sense is not common."

And I suppose he is right. I have a window to the Universe that is very different from most people. It is a window I discovered as a child and through which I Saw and accessed spiritual realms. Many of my current clients are surprised to discover that my unique perspectives and gifts began and continue to be nurtured through Catholic Mass.

While Sunday Mass is part of all Catholic experience, my mother attended daily, in the wee hours of the morning, while my father readied for work before the children arose. At six years old, when I first joined my mother at daily Mass, it was the desire for one-on-one time with her that motivated me to get out of bed at six in the morning. Here was a unique, precious opportunity that did not include the presence of my then-seven siblings in competition for her time and affection.

I peered up at the altar from the pew that came to my chin as I knelt next to my mother. While for some church can feel cold and daunting, from the first time I entered, it all felt familiar, from the stained-glass windows to the priests in their robes to the celebration of the Mass. I felt happy there.

Even at that very young age, I felt immediately drawn to Christ in that natural way so many children do when the God of their faith tradition is described to them. It was as if this relationship had been waiting for me to remember it. In fact, when the priest lifted the chalice at what is called "the consecration of the Mass," I had a strong, visceral, familiar feeling that sent shivers down my spine. I said to my six-year-old self, "I know how to do that."

It was not long before church became the place where I could direct my anxieties, fears, and hopes. It was a place in which my spirit could move freely, and where I felt more space for my thoughts and feelings than sometimes seemed possible in my happy yet very busy home life. Rather than competing for the stage with my gregarious and funny siblings, I found I had God's time and attention.

In silent conversation, I could actually run out of things to say…and then we just stared at each other. I felt at peace—first, perhaps, because I found a place where I felt seen, heard, and understood; later, because that place began to offer me experiences I could find nowhere else.

After a few years of daily Mass, when I received Communion, I found myself jettisoned into a powerful and intense Light that even as a child I called "the realm where words no longer have meaning." I felt infinitely safe and protected there. I used to think, "If everyone could know how much they are loved, how very precious each person is to God, they would never feel afraid of anything, and they would want to give and share everything they had."

To know this Light is to know joy. The assumption of richness is so palpable in this Light that nothing is out of reach. Miracles might be called its way of being. There is no corollary, no metaphor, no state of mind on earth that resembles it. It is unnamable.

Although I was a child, I felt old, like so many youth seem today— "an old soul." My commitment to Christ was founded upon this innocent maturity that could only partly be located in my biological age. I knew that I wanted nothing more than to cultivate an intimate and devoted friendship with the One whose Voice felt like Home to me.

Indeed it was this relationship that was at the heart of my silent response to my third-grade teacher's question: "What do you want to be when you grow up?" While some of my fellow students raised their hands high and excitedly listed artist, doctor, and astronaut, I remained quiet, knowing my answer would not be well received.

A priest once made it clear to our class that girls could not grow up and enter the priesthood. Despite this rule, after carefully observing the priest's role and actions every day at Mass, I felt a certainty within. I did not say to myself, "Someday I want to be a priest." Instead, I clearly remember thinking, "I am a priest."

Even as a child, I could tell that some priests related to their vocation as though it were a job, which they faithfully fulfilled, one task at a time…and I thought, "These are not priests."

Later in life I concluded that some of us are called to priesthood— not the job or position of priest but a priesthood of the heart and soul whose ordination comes by birth rather than rules that determine what gender or description is best qualified to serve. In any case, I have always thought of my abilities—which sometimes showed up unbidden—as gifts of the Holy Spirit. As I grew in these gifts, I thought of them purely as priestly gifts, given for the purpose of serving both individuals and organizations.

Without being conferred robes to officially get about the business of offering my gifts to a community, I spent decades searching for a place or way to employ them for the highest good. I wandered the world as a "mystic without a monastery," as author Caroline Myss describes it. While still a child, I simply prayed to be of service and allowed my gifts to emerge in that spirit.

Throughout grammar school, being lifted into the Light at church was an experience that continued unabated. In those eternal moments, I learned what it meant to be in relationship with Oneness. I Saw how all things and people are interconnected, how startlingly beloved each person is within the Light, and how we all belong to the Light.

At the age of nine, as I was about to sit down after kneeling at church, I found myself suddenly frozen between the two positions. I felt a powerful force pick me up, and a Voice with enormous fierceness said, "If I but blinked and forgot you, you would cease to exist!" I felt an awesome and frightening Presence, and was terrified at its enormity. Then, at exactly the same moment, I Heard the same Almighty Power softly say, "And I love you so dearly, I would never forget you."

This was a juxtaposition of might and gentleness: of the complete control Spirit seems to have over our lives and the complete freedom of will the Creator has given us. This is the God I came to know— paradoxical, mysterious, complete.

TESTING: WHOSE REALITY DO YOU TRUST?

I was blessed to develop my unusual spirit through the privacy of my intimate connection with Christ. On rare occasions, I would "Hear" that it was safe to talk about my faith experiences with particular others. For the most part, however, I kept this relationship growing in the dark and stillness of my own soul.

I found "Communion" a wise choice of words for my experience of receiving the Eucharist at Mass, and the Voice of Christ became my constant companion. I began to understand everything outside of me as practice and application for developing what I was learning from my inner spiritual relationship. I was devoted throughout elementary school years to following His guidance, which helped me with eventually making sense of different elements I encountered in the invisible realms. The guidance started with simple things.

I "Heard," for example, that it was important to stay detached from all things human. Therefore I performed such "monumental" acts as allowing my six carnivorous brothers to have second helpings at dinner without trying to grab the food from their hands before it landed on their plates. I let them tease me about the dessert I wouldn't eat because I was "giving it up" for a particular spiritual intention, in imitation of my very self-disciplined mother.

Sometimes I struggled, feeling the urge and right to claim even my favorite teacup. With every release of a desire that I surrendered in favor of neutrality, however, I felt stronger and more aware of life from an inner lens. Often I felt sheer joy in the freedom from attachment.

Listening deeply to inner guidance encouraged me to see through things and into their meaning. Faith meant seeing what was in front of me, but not necessarily believing it.

My faith was tested in ordinary situations. By way of example, my mother taught us that if we wanted God's help at school, we should "pray as if praying were the only thing, study like studying was the only thing, and leave the rest to God." After praying and studying particularly hard for a science test, it was returned to me with a C grade. I felt angry with God, knowing I had done my part in both studying and praying for a good grade! After reflecting on those feelings, I decided that if I lived by faith, I would have to accept that this was the best possible outcome, despite all appearances to the contrary. I was aware that this was not how I truly felt inside, but I insisted to myself that I would believe it anyway.

At lunch hour, I went to the church attached to my Catholic grammar school. Kneeling down, I explained to God that even though I felt angry with Him, I had faith that He must have done everything He could, despite my C grade. I felt awkward and ridiculous as I urged myself to keep believing that everything was perfect as it was, despite the obvious outcome. I thanked Him and promised to move on and think of it no more.

When I returned from lunch, I was horrified that the teacher insisted on going over the test in every detail with the whole class. Holding my nauseous stomach at bay, I dutifully faced what I considered my failure. As Mrs. Kendall read each answer aloud, I slowly realized that she had mismarked one answer after another. Afterward, when I showed her the test, she re-marked it, apologized, and gave me an A. As I walked back to my seat, I Heard the God of my Heart say, "And that wasn't the only test you just passed."

I understood that this spiritual test was asking me, "Can you believe that your prayers are answered beyond the evidence that clearly and factually shows you the opposite?"

DIVINE TIMING IS EVERYTHING

Another time I acted on faith instead of believing in clear evidence was when my father came home particularly exhausted one evening after a long day at work. Dad's income as a dentist was responsible for all eleven of us attending Catholic high schools and then onto college.

My father was a man of few words, and I never heard him complain or voice distress. However, on that evening, I sensed there was something amiss.

"Is everything OK, dad?"

Slowly and softly my dad replied, "I just spent two weeks training Janice, my new assistant. We agreed on the hours she would work and we were all set to go." He sighed heavily. "Today Janice called to say she received her class schedule in the mail. Her classes will not allow her to work the hours we agreed to. So I have to start over."

As I watched him slowly walk upstairs, I turned to my mother and said: "I'll pray for Dad. Things will be OK in twenty-four hours."

My mother was taken aback. "God loves each of us and listens to each prayer, honey. Whatever time the prayer is answered is the right time."

"He will answer this one *now*, Mom, I know it," I said, feeling fervently convinced that God would want to make my dear, hardworking father's path less burdened.

Mom said gently, "Therese, God answers prayers in His time. Prayer does not make God do our will. Prayer helps us to align with His will. We pray, 'Thy will be done.'"

"Yes, that's true, Mom. But in this case, both people, Dad and his assistant, want the same thing. Their will is aligned, and what they want is for the good of all. So it will be done."

My good and caring mother left it at that, seeing that I was determined.

I ran upstairs, closed my bedroom door, knelt down, and prayed with fervor. In *The Isaiah Effect*, Gregg Branden describes a kind of prayer outlined in the ancient texts that had been kept by monks in the high mountains of Tibet for centuries. The texts describe how the Essene culture practiced prayer. In one part, they said it was important to include one's feelings in line with a single-minded intention for another.

When I read that passage, I was struck by the similarity of this description to my own way of praying. First, I moved into the "sincerest part of my heart." There, I would passionately feel my love for the person for whom I was praying, and imagined the intensity of God's love for me and for them. Then I willed with all my might for the ending I wanted or for which others had asked me to pray. Finally, as my mother suggested, I asked for God's will to be done, since I was aware that I did not have all the information about what is best for a person, and our Creator does.

Because it was my beloved father for whom I prayed, my love found its target quickly and easily. When I finished praying, I went downstairs and said to my mother. "It's done. Things will change in twenty-four hours."

My compassionate mother quietly said, "OK, dear, let's see."

The next day I was upstairs and I heard my mother call. When I arrived at the kitchen table, I found her sitting next to the phone, shaking her head and smiling. "That was Dad on the phone. He wanted to know if we were praying for him. He said that his assistant just got a call from the school saying they had made a mistake on her class schedule. Now she can work the hours she and your father had planned."

It was exactly nineteen hours after I'd prayed.

While I know that when wills align, prayer is made more powerful, I also know that timing is dependent upon many things. Perhaps this was one of those fortunate instances when my hopes and God's time embraced.

WHOSE MAP OF REALITY RULES?

In high school, I was given the opportunity to become aware of where I placed my loyalty, trust, and allegiance when it came to rules and expectations.

There was a small chapel at my school where I became a daily visitor during my free periods. Kneeling down, I prayed and then waited until I felt "released" from my encounters there. Even when I was finished praying, the silence that followed was nourishment for my soul.

I believed Spirit always had my best interest in mind. I had many opportunities to learn that when it was time to leave for class, Spirit would let me know. Indeed, there was a particular feeling that came over me, as if someone who was hugging me tightly had finally put me down.

While kneeling in silence one day, I heard the first bell ring. I opened my eyes to see if I'd missed the signal to go. As I looked at my watch, I Heard the familiar Voice quietly say, "Stay…stay."

I waited, thinking perhaps I would soon receive some profound insight or wisdom. I focused inside my heart and Heard nothing. Then the second bell rang, and despite my growing panic, I Heard again, "Stay."

Obeying, I closed my eyes, knowing that I would, without a doubt, be late for class. I wondered what God was up to—as well as how I would tell the teacher who wanted my excuse, "I'm sorry, but I was waiting for God to tell me it was time to go."

After five more minutes, and without one ounce of profundity, I felt "released." I Heard, "You may go now."

I may go now?! As I quickly tried to invent a plausible excuse for my inevitable tardiness, an indignant part of me thought, "What was that all about?" Another part of me clung to the Gospel words "Seek ye first the Kingdom of God and all else shall follow." I certainly wondered what was to follow.

I walked into class ten minutes late. I looked around to see the teacher working with some students and everyone else busy studying at their tables. I slipped into my chair, and not one person turned toward me. No one looked up; no one questioned me.

Then I Heard the Gospel words "At my name, every head shall bow and every knee shall bend." I also Heard, "I created time and space. Stay attuned to Me, and outer reality will follow." It was a clear and powerful Voice.

Spirit asked me to trust beyond the everyday conventions that are logical, helpful, and necessary to well-organized living. This was the beginning of a practice of attending to the guidance of a higher order in the midst of everyday life. Through my committed practice, subtle signals that emerged from the invisible realm became more prominent than the drone of outer noise, or even the rules of worldly authority.

The practice of listening in at this level was not for the sake of my own desire to shirk the rules (though I had plenty of questions about the sanity and good judgment of some in authority)—but from my loyalty to a relationship with the One who authors all rules.

MANIFESTING THE INVISIBLE REQUEST

The first time I created a program that came to me through prayer and that included many people, I was still only sixteen years old. Back on my familiar kneeler at the chapel, I Heard: "Institutionalize freshman retreats at your school."

At first, I did a double take: "Wait a minute…what?!" And I Heard it again. I had never heard "institution" used as a verb before, but I did understand the reference to freshmen retreats.

A month earlier, I was chosen to be one of the few girl team leaders for weekend freshmen retreat at the all-boy Catholic high school down the road from my school. The order of brothers that ran the school planned every minute of the weekend. At the same time, they took away everyone's watch and covered all the clocks so no one knew what time it was. One of the themes of the retreat was "don't anticipate." Not having access to the agenda or time, freshmen participants had to pay attention in a new way.

The brothers used many methods, including basketball games, structured exercises, and discussions of how to apply lessons from Gospel stories to everyday life, to stimulate students' thinking. Also, the brothers purposely paired up students who didn't know each other, and then switched pairs throughout the weekend, interfering with the formation of any natural groups, such as those who were best at basketball. They assured that unlikely partners got to know each other—from the heart. I realized that they were doing this for freshmen so they could set a foundation for open minds. Kids were also discovering that they might find value and common ground in unexpected friendships.

While understanding this reference to retreats, I didn't have any idea how to "institutionalize" anything, but if Christ said to do it, I would find a way. In preparation, I actually looked up the word "institutionalize" and understood that it meant making something last over time. Calling the executive director (the term we used for "principal") I made an appointment to talk about this.

In most high schools, it would be impossible for a sixteen-year-old to make institutional changes. However, the Mercy nuns ran my school (and still do today), and they were a force to be reckoned with. They counted among their teachers many PhD and master's degree recipients, and their objective was to ready young women for the world ahead of them. As visionaries, they also knew the world was changing, and their most ardent objectives were to forward leadership, values, and critical-thinking skills.

There was a story that characterized the Mercy nuns that took place years before I entered. It was the late sixties, and many schools and parents across the country were meeting to discuss the controversial books that were then available to young people. The books highlighted racial prejudice and contained unsavory language. The Mercy nuns assigned students these books in English classes, and the parents were up in arms. An assembly of angry and concerned parents attended a gathering that the executive director created to discuss the controversy. As was their custom, the Mercy nuns actively and compassionately listened to each parent.

As the story goes, at the end of the assembly, the executive director said to the parents, "Thank you for your comments. We have heard your concerns, and we understand you are anxious about the material being presented in the classrooms. However, we are preparing your girls to be leaders in a world that is now changing. They will need to understand everything about that world to critically think through their choices to make good decisions and contribute their gifts. If that is not the kind of education you want for your child, please take your daughter out of the school." End of meeting.

The courage these teachers demonstrated arose from prayerful conviction. These role models were life affirming for me and shaped my understanding of what was possible for women in the world. Their pioneering, holistic education formed the basis of the work I have done in the world to date.

At my meeting with the executive director, I was direct: "I want to institutionalize freshman retreats. I will create the first retreat. If it is successful, then I want you to institutionalize them."

True to the Mercy nuns' discipline, Sister Bryant did not burst out laughing or even try to hide a smile. She simply asked me to tell her more about what I meant and what I wanted. Describing the all-boy retreat I had team-led, I explained why I thought it was important. I did not tell her I got this idea from the chapel…that would have been way too hard to explain, even to a nun. Sister Bryant told me to put my ideas to paper and then asked if I would be willing to go in front of the executive board to present my idea.

"Of course," I said, as if I had done it a hundred times.

The following week, impervious to the fact that I was the only young person among a long table of adults, I explained my philosophy to the executive board. "The retreats help kids get to know each other and get comfortable talking about God with each other before their egos"—I did use that word—"set in and they start forming cliques and shutting down."

I remember silence and a lot of eyes staring at me. Mr. Janice, a science teacher and board member, made some remarks about expense and extra resources and teachers' extra time. I tried to listen to his remarks, but his voice was muffled under my panic that if they said no, what was I going to tell Jesus?

Immediately when Mr. Janice finished speaking, I passionately said, "This is a Catholic institution, and this retreat represents values consistent with Catholic experience. How can we not do this?"

Sister Bryant thanked me for my presentation as if I were a professional rather than a teenager, and told me they would consider my proposal. I felt fairly treated, but I was really worried that I would have to go back to the chapel having failed my assignment.

The news came the following week: Sister Bryant agreed to let me hold the first retreat. Always going for the goal, I said, "Will you promise me that if the first retreat works out well, you will institutionalize it?"

She said, "I can't promise that, but if it goes well over time, we will consider that." Well, at least I had tried.

In a flurry of activity, I secured a date, organized the agenda, signed up speakers, found a priest to say Mass, solicited parent chaperones, and assured security would be there, as we would be staying in the school overnight. A few underpaid, overworked teachers not only grumbled loudly as the plans moved forward, but then seemed to deliberately put impediments in the way, insisting that the permission slips were not adequate or there were not enough security guards or they wanted more chaperones.

On the basis of whatever inadequacy could be identified, rather than helping me, the teachers insisted the event be canceled again and again. In determined protest, and remembering Who had made the initial request, I showed up every single morning at the door of the director of religious studies, who had authority to give me permission to proceed. When she finally grew tired of me showing up, she gave in.

By this time, the speaker and priest were no longer available. Unwilling to let that stop me, I decided I would be the speaker. I wrote the Mass myself, picked out and recorded the music, designed the exercises and discussions, and was prepared to be a one-person show (minus the priest, whom I finally solicited and secured from a nearby church).

The retreat was a big hit. The students loved it and demanded more. However, I was a wreck. Directly following the weekend, I broke down and cried for two days, and couldn't get out of bed for three days as a result of emotional exhaustion. The next year the administration institutionalized freshmen retreats, and they still exist today.

Later in life I learned other ways to accomplish a goal, including identifying stakeholders, understanding their fears and interests, and working toward the buy-in and the contribution of all involved. At the time, it was simply my determination to be faithful to the Voice within that motivated me to push through like a bull in a china shop. Regardless of the emotional outcome, it strengthened my resolve to prioritize my inner life as the basis for outer action.

REFLECTION

My childhood map of reality was built upon one organizing principle: an intimate and trusting relationship with my Creator. Whatever was requested or taught from that Source, I wanted to learn or do, because, with a fervor that perhaps only a child can possess, I wanted to live these words: "Seek ye first the Kingdom of God, and all else shall follow."

The legend on my map that kept me aligned with my spiritual relationship included:

- Believe without seeing.

- Trust without evidence.

- Obey without question.

CHAPTER TWO

Moving toward a New Reality

It happened when I was fourteen years old, after Mass one Sunday. I often stayed until I was the last person in the church. The silence was exquisite.

It was then that I Heard, "Things will be different between us when you are twenty-one." This frightened me. I asked frantically what that meant.

"How different? How will things change?"

My questions were answered by silence. As is true of many times in the mystery of life, I could only carry this Knowing with me as lightly as possible and without further explanation or insight. By the time I packed my bags for college, I forgot all about this clear impression.

THERE ARE NO "WRONG CHOICES"

When I took my first introductory college course in psychology, I was thrilled. I called it "ministry in motion." To learn a profession in which I would be able to help people mine the wisdom of their inner selves seemed the next best thing to priesthood. However, in my second year, one of my brothers advised me that I could make no money in the real world with a degree in psychology and that I should study business.

With a sense of responsibility for making my own way in the world, I shifted my loyalty from the study of inner guidance to the rational analytics that defined the language of the marketplace. I abruptly changed majors, loading my semester with computer science, accounting, economics, finance, and organizational behavior.

By finals time that semester, I had severe stomachaches. The infirmary doctor oddly prescribed muscle relaxers and put me on a fast of Jell-O and water for a week. In this state I took finals. Despite my good grasp of most of the subjects, the words swam back and forth on the exams. I predictably did miserably. The body cannot lie: I could not stomach my new direction.

My parents visited me at college for the first and only time. My father took one look at me, and rather than addressing my diet, he insisted I change my major back to psychology. A wise father is a rare thing (and one who trusts his intuition, even rarer).

I was very grateful for his insistence that I follow my initial passion. He had always encouraged us to major in whatever subject was most interesting to us, suggesting that earning the degree was the most important part. Then if we wanted to specialize, there was always graduate school.

And so I returned to my first love, psychology. The good that came from a painful dunk in subjects related to "the real world" was the discovery of another love: organizational behavior.

In addition to organizational behavior's focus of applying psychology within the structured environment of business, I had an opportunity to begin to learn more about the nature of the marketplace. Perhaps business reminded me of my well-organized family.

My mother and father were two gifted leader-partners. There was great consideration given to each child's individual needs and motivations. We worked in rotating, assigned teams to do chores. My father even let me believe that I helped him develop a point system for allowance, or rewards for work accomplished. (I was elated to be the point taker with the accompanying extra reward—and no one else wanted the job.)

Undoubtedly, it was the long-standing experience of living into my family's model of organization and community, more than my later Northwestern Kellogg MBA, that prepared me for the large-scale change work I would later do with business leaders. In college, I decided to mix the curricula of psychology and business, graduating a semester early, one course short of a double major.

"GOD, MAKE HIM DO HIS HUMAN HOMEWORK!"

Life at the university became my next context for spiritual learning. I once dated a man who was not of my religious tradition. As our relationship progressed, I began to notice the differences in our approaches to our respective faiths. I went to daily prayer group and Mass as often as possible, volunteered because I loved it and it was part of my faith, and consciously worked on my spiritual life.

Jerry didn't pray, go to church in any formal way, or work on his inner life. Yet I observed that he was more patient and humble than me. Without thinking, he put others' needs before his own. He acted out of integrity, honesty, kindness, and love. Jerry was a deeply good person.

After I while, I began to compare our spiritual "workloads." It felt as if I were doing six hours of homework every night for an entire semester to earn an B+, while Jerry, "the kid next to me," got to walk into the final exam with a hangover, never having cracked a book, and still received the better grade. Entirely unfair! I asked God why Jerry didn't seem to have to work so hard for his faith.

"How is it that he does a minimum of spiritually conscious work and is still such a good person?" (here read "better than me"). In a word, I was jealous.

I Heard Christ say, "Do not question how I come to others. That is between each person and Me. Only know and remember that I come to you in the 'breaking of the bread.'"

By that I understood He meant for me to be faithful to our relationship that came to me through Holy Communion at Mass where my mystic road began. As for what was true for others, His message was clear: stop evaluating and judging. No one can know another person's relationship with the Divine.

While this response did not abate my jealousy, I felt the authority of this Love that honored each person's uniqueness and did not seek to manipulate or to insist on a uniform salute to earn Spirit's attention. Jerry's portal to the Divine was not wired or exercised the same way as mine, and his did not require the kind of vigilance I felt called to practice. Yet, Jerry was as uniquely and dearly loved as I knew I was.

Jerry was the first person who taught me about the beauty and uniqueness of each person's path. Years later I knew that if everyone could perceive energetically and spiritually the way I could, the only possible response to how others access the Divine would be profound respect and to take off your shoes—because no matter how different it is from your experience, you are standing on Holy Ground.

WHEN THE INNER VOICE GOES SILENT

I had many other tests that enhanced the strength of my faith. However, my direct access to daily conversations and lessons with Spirit were about to end.

One day around my twenty-first birthday, I woke up, and it seemed all at once as though someone had flipped a dimmer switch and all the color in the world had slipped away.

I attended my usual prayer meeting that day in hopes of shaking off this feeling, and was shocked to discover that I had somehow forgotten how to pray! Although I had always been an active participant, I couldn't think of a thing to add when it was my turn to pray aloud. When I listened to others, it was as if they were speaking in a foreign tongue. I panicked.

The only thing that felt familiar were the Bible passages as read by a friend of mine from Nigeria named Tobi. When he spoke from the Gospels in his beautiful Nigerian accent, it was as if they were common stories that his mother had told him at breakfast that day.

At the end of the meeting, I quietly asked him if he would meet with me and teach me more about the Bible. Although my Bible had tattered pages with multicolored, underlined passages, I suddenly felt like a neophyte. Without even a question as to why I would have such an interest, he graciously agreed. When I visited him the next day, I remember literally sitting at his feet in rapt attention. Every time he spoke a sentence, I felt as though someone had placed a drop of water on my parched tongue.

"This is what it means, Therese. You see, a man is put in jail, and he knows he has done wrong so he does not fight it. Then, here comes Jesus. 'You are free, my friend,' He says, 'Come out of jail now.' And the door swings open.

"But the man will not come out.

"'Come out. It is fine. I forgive you. All is well,' Jesus says.

"'No, I cannot come out,' replies the man. 'I am a bad man. It is not right that I should come out.'

"'Please,' Jesus replies, 'I love you dearly. Run to Me. I will help you. It will be OK now.'

"'I am too ashamed,' says the man.

"And so on and on they go. Jesus begs the man to come to Him, and the man keeps saying he cannot forgive himself. That is what it means, Therese. We keep doing that. Hiding from the love that is waiting for us."

I returned again and again to hear Tobi tell me about Jesus's love, yet these drops of holy water were not enough to restore my spiritual sensibilities. I felt empty and blank inside.

Finally wondering if this might be more than a temporary condition, I ran to Mass and prayed fervently. "Have I done something wrong? Am I not volunteering enough? Not praying enough?" I would do anything to recover my spiritual gifts. Having forgotten that when I was fourteen years old Christ had said that our relationship would change, I thought I must have inadvertently done something to cause this darkness.

This is what I Heard in response: "You did not earn these gifts, and you cannot earn them back. Your gifts are Mine to give and Mine to hold." I was stunned. Did that mean the rest of my life would be like this—without color or the intimate Presence of the Spirit that felt so familiar?

"What should I do then?" I asked Him miserably. The response was clear: "Read the book *The Autobiography of St. Teresa of Avila*." That was it.

The only thing I knew of Teresa of Avila was that she was a saint who was considered the first woman doctor of the Church, and a mystic.

I had learned a little about mysticism through reading about Catholic saints, some of whose descriptions of their encounters with the Divine were suspiciously similar to mine. When one of my teachers talked about mysticism, it felt like she was talking about Home. I was also aware that this worldview was very different than those who had built their faith on dogma—that is, those who focused on the authoritative rules of the Church.

My first learning about the difference between mystically and dogmatically based perspectives came when I was in high school. I had joined a local prayer group. I was happy with their emphasis on the power of prayer and on an intimate relationship with Christ.

At one point, they began to talk about who was going to hell and who would go to heaven as though they had the definitive Divine scoop. I was appalled, feeling defensive on behalf of the God of my Heart.

"The God I know," I said defiantly, "would not condemn those who have found other ways to learn about love than the one we accept." In response, they showed me Biblical passages they held as proof that their ideas were sacrosanct. Despite the authority of their references, I felt unspeakably angry that anyone could think that God's love is exclusive. I abruptly left.

Over the years, I have grown to understand that these participants were loyal to the dogma of the Church, and therefore had a strong sense of who and what is "right" and "wrong," "good" and "evil." I understood this more clearly when I heard another story about the difference between beliefs grounded in the mystic and those grounded in dogma.

One summer, a Christian/Buddhist conference was held in Colorado. The participants sought common ground despite their unique paradigms of spiritual devotion. Those who were "keepers of the dogma" on both sides seemed to have little to discuss. They broke into logically assigned groups to talk about the similarities and differences of their sacred texts and interpretations, and struggled toward shared understanding.

Meanwhile, the mystics in both traditions were a lively group, finding little need to work or struggle. Instead, they quickly found common ground in their strikingly similar descriptions of their connection to Oneness and the Divine.

Likewise, in her autobiography, Saint Teresa of Avila says that we are all part of the whole. In the Light common to mystics, there are no divisions, no better or worse, no judgments—only openness, mercy, compassion, ever-unfolding understanding, and forgiveness. Being disciplined in prayer and detachment, mystics can stay aligned with the Truth that they Know. Over time they learn to discern the spiritual meaning that lives under everyday reality. This requires devotion to listening into the subtle promptings of Spirit.

As I read Saint Teresa's accounts of her world and listened to the Buddhist/Christian Conference story, I wondered if I had been in mystic training for my entire childhood. Indeed, I held dear this map of reality. At that time, it was a happy revelation to know that I was not alone in my uncommon experiences of the Light.

Now, however, I felt an outsider to the sensibilities that used to be "normal" for me. It felt as if I had been sentenced to traversing the dark side of a painfully steep mountain without a map.

As I read on, Saint Teresa addressed my discomfort as she wrote about a period of time that her close friend and later fellow saint, John of the Cross, called "The Dark Night of the Soul."

Saint Teresa described it as a dry, desert-like experience, where access to joy is absent, the precise opposite of the ecstasy of Oneness. The spiritual realms that typically provide great inner richness and comfort are not accessible during this time. It is a period of darkness and unknowing. It requires true faith, because there are no assurances or signs that one is moving forward on the path of God's will.

The more I read, the heavier my heart felt, as I became convinced my "spiritual amnesia" was the onset of this season of faith. However, I had no idea what to do about it. Naming something makes it feel "real" but provides no map for fixing, helping, or curing it. In fact, each season of faith progresses us to the next unknown, not back to the place from which we just emerged.

There is a loss here. It marks an ending that must somehow be grieved, and then released, to make room for what is to come.

I have since learned that the Dark Night takes us on "the road less traveled" and offers us an education that would not be possible if we clung to the map of reality we most want or enjoy.

In my typical driven way, I decided to buck up under this dark weight. My only question was, "How long will I have to endure this test?" I had not experienced anything like it in my life, but having great determination, I planned to buckle down, use my laser-like focus, and figure this out—or just get through it.

I was not at all prepared for the hollowness of this season. Along with the absence of color, it was like the deep notes and harmonies were gone from the sound of life. To my long-trained ear, I now heard a cacophony of clanging sounds without the director of the symphony present to tap his wand and bring the instruments to attention and synchronization.

I could not Hear into the meaning of what people said. I could not See the symbolic meaning of what I read. I could not access the fabric of spiritual material that I used before to weave together the threads of life's lessons. I felt alone, and for the first time, lonely.

Without the Light that animated my life as well as my sense of purpose and direction, I felt a kind of fragmentation that I began to suspect most people daily experience.

From the perspective of Oneness, making life-giving choices just makes sense. From the fractured perspective that we are all separate, I slowly began to understand why people make other kinds of choices. I was reexamining even the basics.

MEANING IN THE DARK: MONEY AND SEX

At twenty-one, as I stepped into the world as most people know it, I understood for the first time how people thought money was important. Prior to that time, money was a means of doing God's will. When I needed it for a project, I would simply ask for what was required and had complete confidence it would come. It would arrive promptly, just as clearly as all the gurus of positive affirmations assure.

For example, one time I asked God for one hundred dollars needed for a service project that I was directing in college. Within a week of that prayer, I was on an airplane on my way to see a friend, and happened to be seated next to a businessman. In my youthful enthusiasm, I blathered on with stories about my life, my faith, and my volunteer work. When I returned from a restroom break, the man handed me an envelope.

"What is this?" I asked.

He replied, "Don't open it until you get off the plane."

I frowned and wondered what he was up to. The envelope was thick, and as I held it up to the light, I could see it contained cash.

Feeling the bright red heat of my cheeks, I handed it back to him. "I can't take your money," I declared, as I scanned my memory for any hint I might have given him that I was in need.

He insisted as he handed it back, "I'm not going to tell you my name or anything about myself. I want you to take this money and use it for your project. Someday, when you are older, you will make money, and it will be your turn to give it to someone else."

Although I was certain I had not mentioned money to this man, the envelope contained exactly one hundred dollars. I was deeply grateful and moved by his generosity—and it was then that I remembered my prayer. Ah yes, God was using this man's good heart to bring needed resources to a project dedicated to the service of others! My mystic understanding of our interconnectedness made this incident feel like "common sense." These kinds of "direct prayer responses" were ordinary to my experience.

After the Dark Night ensued, however, money got confusing, as it suddenly seemed separate from Spirit. I could actually fathom the idea of making money for its own sake. Yet I knew that money without purpose was only valuable for what insecurity it could mask. And the most essential reason for feeling insecure in the world was the sense of being disconnected from Spirit.

I likened this disconnect to the relationship between love and sex: when they are one, sex is an expression of love, and communion or unity is possible. When we separate them, there is an eventual feeling of emptiness from sex for its own sake. Anything that is disconnected from its Source is unfulfilling.

GIFT OR PATHOLOGY?

I felt frightened and lost, but I had to decide what direction to take as I headed for graduate school. I considered graduate school in psychology. Since my father recommended returning to psychology as a major, I had taken many more courses and had become dismayed and disappointed that psychology insisted on categorizing and labeling people by their pathologies rather than by their giftedness. Spirit had never prompted me to help someone by focusing on his weaknesses.

Listening to others voice difficult feelings, compassionately trying to understand the context of them, and then supporting them to find their strength and sense of self is one process. Deciding that someone is a label, such as "he is a depressed person," and then "helping" someone based on that identity is entirely another. Ironically, I found little consciousness in the field of psychology. It seemed to treat people as nouns, forever fixed with labels—the best label being "normal."

I thought of people as God's verbs, which have eternal evolution, with the constant possibility of remembering that they are loved and whole. My heart broke whenever a label discouraged or dismissed the Spirit's potential for breaking through to new life.

So rather than continue to submit my spiritual intuition to a map of reality based on pathology, I decided to follow another path in graduate school.

Without knowing exactly where to focus for next steps, I applied to the MBA program at the University of Illinois, as well as for a master's in public administration focused in marketing for nonprofit organizations at the University of Denver. Having volunteered for two years as a public relations director for the largest volunteer organization at the University of Illinois, I had begun consulting with other campus organizations. Specifically, I was working to help them focus public relations efforts through marketing and fundraising. I was pleasantly surprised to learn that the University of Denver offered a master's degree in the area of not-for-profit organizations. Though accepted to both places, based on timing and scholarship money, I decided to go to Denver.

During graduate school, while still praying through my Dark Night without much response, my spiritual experiences began to take on a new twist, and my map of reality began to burst at the seams.

REFLECTION

When the Dark Night fell, I felt altogether lost. The heart of my understanding of life was gone, leaving behind letters (like sacred texts and faith-filled friends) that recalled what I used to Hear the God of my Heart say to me. This was the death of a way of life. No letters would bring back the feelings of intimacy I had known. Being directed to read *The Autobiography of St. Teresa of Avila* was like being pointed in the direction of the priest or minister sitting just outside the hospital room door...after finally being willing to admit that this is the appropriate time for last rites or final prayers.

My map of reality would surely have to change, but how? My analytic brain tried to abate my sense of helplessness in a striking new world where façades replaced authentic meaning.

However, it would be the Dark Night itself that would become my unwanted guide in a transformative process whose journey and end point I could not yet imagine.

CHAPTER THREE

"Shirley, I Can Read Energy"

After the Dark Night commenced, new realities intruded upon my everyday experience when I came home between semesters from graduate school to visit my boyfriend. His mother was watching a variety show in which Shirley MacLaine was the featured actress. Mrs. Daley asked me to sit with her and watch television for a while. To be polite, I reluctantly agreed, not admitting that I'd rather be out with her son. As I watched, I started to feel my abdomen spin. Then I began to babble. I pointed at the television screen and said with great angst, "There is something wrong with that woman!"

Mrs. Daley was taken aback. "What are you talking about? She's just dancing!"

I was focused on my abdomen as though I were reading it like a book. "No, there's something very wrong. She is going through something right now that is so important, if she doesn't figure it out, if she doesn't get it, she could die." I was mortified at my nonsensical words, but I could not help the surge, from the intense feeling to the words.

This was foreshadowing of how I would later "Read" energy. The words formulate and then stream in without my ego's evaluation of their relevance or appropriateness to the situation. Certainly they make no accommodations for the sense of humiliation that follows!

Immediately I said, "I have to go!" Abruptly I ran outside, around and around the block, until the overwhelming energy dissipated. It was the year Shirley MacLaine had begun to experience the events she would later pen in her first book, *Out on a Limb*. Without any language or understanding of it at the time, I was essentially "Reading" Shirley MacLaine's energy through the television screen and could feel the enormity of her path. Her story would serve the world by opening doors to new thought—a world I would not explore until after I spent a few years in the "real world."

COLLECTIVE FIELDS IN THE "REAL WORLD"

When I returned from Denver with master's degree in hand, I knew exactly where I wanted to go. Since I could not be a priest, I was determined to work with the Church in another capacity. I had my eyes set on managing a Sister City Project with the Archdiocese of Chicago. It was a program that connected overseas communities with those in Chicago for the purpose of cultural and resource exchange. I felt happily prepared to fulfill my sense of purpose until I ran headlong into the Catholic Church's personnel map of reality.

The cardinal handily turned down my application because, as his assistant related, "The cardinal doesn't hire women." End of conversation. It never occurred to me that this journey would be such a short trip! The Catholic map of reality was again too small to welcome my gifts in the way I wanted to share them.

Subsequently I interviewed many nonprofit organizations and began to see that their maps were focused on great care and respect for clients, but did not value structure, accountability, or financial balance.

At one point, a reference to Notre Dame University brought me into contact with Father John Egan, assistant to then-president Reverend Theodore Hesburgh. I was frank about my feelings regarding the nonprofit sector, and I told Father Egan that the cardinal would not hire me at the Archdiocese because I am a woman.

Father Egan gently joked, "Therese, don't take that personally. It's not that the cardinal doesn't like women; it's that he doesn't like people."

Father Egan hoped I could run a new national project for which he was waiting for funding. When the money did not come through, he suggested I explore business. "The nonprofit sector will always be here," he said, smiling, just as clearly as Christ said, "The poor will be with us always."

"How ironic," I thought, "that a Catholic priest is sending me into the marketplace." Since I wasn't sure where to start, I began in the most counterintuitive fashion I knew.

I asked myself, "Where do I have the least experience and greatest fear?"

The answer came swiftly: "Money." Given my frustration and wonder at the nonprofit sector's lack of attention to this area, this also made sense. So I headed straight into that unknown territory, and was accepted as a management trainee at a bank.

I did not notice this theme for many years, but looking back, it is obvious that I am attracted to and attract people, leaders, businesses, and industries undergoing significant change—the kind of change that offers an opportunity to claim greater wholeness from the inside out.

The banking industry, long known for its staunch stability, was going through major transformation. Working as a management trainee, I had the opportunity to discover and contribute to a number of areas in need of improvement. Within a year and a half, I had researched, recommended, and implemented many significant projects, including the first marketing and electronic funds transfer strategy for ATMs, a bank-wide word-processing system that interfaced with data processing, and a comprehensive recommendation to improve productivity through a new blend of technology and human resources.

Each project resulted in tangible changes that impacted many lives within the organization and for clients. I realized that rather than becoming a banker, I was becoming a consultant. I decided that I wanted to contribute to sweeping changes on an ongoing basis, rather than settle into a banking position.

"A LITTLE BIT HIGHER NOW"

Soon I was hired at one of the top six consulting firms. I was thrilled at the prospect of participating in large-scale change! With a friendly smile, I began my first day, looking forward to meeting new colleagues.

In short order, it became clear that the atmosphere here felt tight. More specifically, there was a sense of pressure that was in high contrast to the freedom, respect, and appreciation I enjoyed in the midsize bank. This company's energy could be more likened to a military outpost—in which I was only one of a handful of women in a platoon of men. It felt as thick an old boys' network as the Papacy—only they let me in. Men made the decisions, held the important positions, and dictated the rewards.

As is now well-known about the rules of the eighties' business map of reality, the unspoken understanding was that women should be grateful to be accepted into the boy's club. They should work harder, be smarter, but understand that they would not be allowed to succeed or go too far. True to this map, I was brought in at a lower salary and position than men who had less education and experience than I did.

At the firm, the rules of engagement were not spoken, but it was easy to feel how important certain behaviors were to progress and succeed. How did everyone seem to know what to do when no one overtly named the expectations?

Through witnessing the contrast between the bank and the consulting firm, I began to understand that there is an unspoken energy at work in a collective organization, and it impacts every part of the work and its outcomes. In this firm, I observed a different kind of leadership than the less formal, more empowering, and mutually respectful one I experienced at the bank. Here I witnessed that the men in charge—and they were all men—were stiff, formal, and often benevolent. Yet when expectations were in jeopardy of being met, internal relationships could include shouting, condescension, and belittling.

I watched and learned. I was a bit horrified at the behavior I observed, yet if I'd replied meekly or politely in certain situations, I would have simply been run over by the "why isn't it here, now?" and "because I'm in charge and I'm important" messages. I slowly formulated a set of behaviors that were responsive to this culture, including tough boundaries that felt righteously protective. I began to imitate to survive.

This was my first exposure to a heady (and I do mean "head-y") top-flight company. It was also my first foray into learning about how the unspoken energy—what I began to call the "Collective Force"—of an environment could overcome even the staunchest, single-minded determination to behave in a way that is different than what was being modeled.

While I was often trying to figure out how to respond to the subtle and not-so-subtle hostility toward women, I also observed the behavior of the partners and thought, "This must be how one is supposed to behave in this sort of company."

Many years later I thought about how often leaders are unaware that they are making sometimes lifelong impressions on young minds with their attitude, what they pay attention to, and their unconscious choice of behavior.

At that time, however, this culture was mirrored by most companies as well as other societal institutions, from medicine to education to government. There were few, if any, successful examples of alternative leadership styles or environments.

With just a little intuitive intelligence or "street smarts," it becomes easy to figure out how to win the game of fitting in, gaining approval, and increasing position and outer wealth—whether in school, work, or personal relationships. Being rewarded for "the win," it becomes easier and easier to avoid confronting personal fears.

Perceptions of unethical behavior become less obvious in an environment where "everybody does it that way." I believe that is why whole companies and industries can become corrupt, as is the case in many companies along Wall Street these days, while those inside remain loyally unaware of other options.

So I learned to be tough and talk tough. When the "old boys" yelled at me, I yelled back. I mirrored their rudeness, their insensitivity, their callousness, and strangely enough, earned their respect. I was assigned to a project which required me to work closely with a particularly cantankerous officer.

Once he telephoned me at my cubicle about a project. When I answered, I could hear him click over to his speakerphone. He began grilling me about work that was past due, and I could hear others in the office with him. He ruled by fear and intimidation, and I knew he was deliberately trying to embarrass me and that this wasn't personal—it was just his way.

Mirroring his style, I shot back the things he owed me that I needed in order to fulfill his request. I knew this would embarrass him, especially with others in the room. I was neither subtle nor humble, but I was polite. Sure enough, he immediately turned off the speakerphone and quickly completed the call. When those in his office left, he yelled for me to come into his office. He was livid that I would "talk back." He said, "Don't ever do that to me again!"

Standing my ground, I firmly replied: "I'll make you a deal. You don't try that with me again, and I won't do that with you again."

I was shocked when he actually backed down. He stopped for a moment, and said, more quietly than his usual shout, "OK."

In my next performance review, he seemed almost nostalgic when he told me I reminded him of himself when he was my age. I was secretly rolling my eyes as I realized that I was imitating this whole dysfunctional environment, and now I was being complimented for "getting it." I was certainly "winning" as much as a woman was allowed to win. And I suddenly knew this didn't feel right.

Despite that feeling, I squirmed and disagreed with myself, at a complete loss to understand another way to survive this environment. While friends I knew who did not work in business found the marketplace a cauldron of political intrigue and irresponsibility, I found business intellectually breathtaking.

I loved the depth and breadth of the work. Many brilliant minds pondered the possibilities for new and old industries, and how to make leaders and companies more effective. It was deeply satisfying to have leading-edge resources at my disposal to gather business information. When data could be effectively analyzed, and findings and conclusions reached, specific recommendations might change the nature of a whole company's direction.

I did not yet know that bringing greater insight and wisdom to a change process and supporting new directions were key to my calling. I did know that I felt an intense conflict between the thrill of contributing to positive change from industry to industry and the pressure of the oppressive culture in which this experience was housed.

It is interesting to note how this situation imitated my experience of Catholicism: the deep wonder of mystic experience with the Divine housed inside a hierarchy of men who could not honor women or their natural, connective contribution. The message was clear in both places:

"What you love, what you can best contribute, and what brings you the most positive energy is here, but you are only welcome in small doses and in particular roles."

In addition, the Dark Night had taken my once whole and interconnected world and had fragmented it. I didn't realize that my consulting work was invisibly connected to my spiritual challenge at the time, but later it became clear. The most essential function of consulting is to investigate fragments and connect them into a meaningful whole so the client company can step up to its more expanded and informed self.

As my friend, Diane, once said to me, "No matter what you are doing, you are always doing your work."

At the consulting firm, emotional survival was the most important focus, and I was still entirely unaware that I had anything to learn from my dilemma. So I leaned into the conflict and just kept going. Even as I applied the many analytical tools of the consulting trade to the engagements, my other gifts leaked. The speed of my intuition was sometimes a challenge.

When a vice president told me to count to ten before I offered a response to client questions, I was concerned.

"Why? Am I giving inaccurate responses?"

He replied: "No, that's not it. It's just that no client believes that you can come up with the right answer so quickly—even when you do. It looks better for the firm if you pretend it took you longer to come up with the answer. By the way," he lectured as though he were a wise elder, "leave your emotions at home. Consultants don't have emotions."

I could have sworn I heard him say, "Women belong at home."

I was quickly being influenced by this company's Collective Force to move from the inner compass and authority of the interconnected and boundless state of mystic experience to the authority of the masculine structures that separate life into categories, rules and tasks.

The firm asked me to complete an MBA, so my nights were filled with Northwestern Kellogg classes in between traveling and working. While most of the MBA subject matter was familiar from my first master's program, the sheer volume of work was overwhelming. Classes and homework were ample additions to the grueling pace and expectations of the firm.

Once while working on a logistics engagement at Federal Express in Memphis, my project manager gave me permission to fly back to Chicago for an MBA class one night a week, but I had to be back by morning and not let the client know. The seven a.m. breakfast meetings were as clear a stipulation for good performance as were the nightly client dinners that dragged on till midnight.

During this three-month project, I developed walking pneumonia. The doctor gave me antibiotics, and I informed the project manager of my health.

He said, "That's awful. OK, take your lunch by the pool in the hotel today"—rather than at the client's offices—"but be back on site by one p.m."

Needless to say, recovery was long in coming. In this Collective Force, time off for illness, unless it was life threatening, was simply not an option.

The loneliness grew as I traveled five days a week for months at a time, with a team of men who were easily on average twenty years older than me. I never worked with another woman. I was often home less than forty-eight hours on weekends. My exhausting schedule often meant I was at the airport at five thirty a.m.

One day I was so tired, I didn't notice that I went into the airport men's room by mistake. Being in one's own world is an interesting phenomenon. Here's the thought that went through my head: "Now why would they put urinals in the women's bathroom?" Shaking my head at the absurdity, I went into the stall.

It wasn't until I was washing my hands and I heard a little boy shout, "Mommy, there's a girl in the boy's bathroom!" that I figured out why the urinals were there.

It seemed an apt metaphor for my life—the only girl in the men's room.

Even though the work schedule was arduous, I witnessed in this company's map of reality an extraordinary efficiency and effectiveness. Ignoring their own and each other's feelings, structuring every task and person into a replaceable box, and spelling out orders in one-way communication in trade for high pay can produce quick and clean results.

I respected the value of aligning operations to meet bottom-line results. Consultants who could quickly analyze and problem solve to get the right answer represented real worth to client companies. I integrated this style into my own, and within a year of working there, especially among colleagues and friends, I acquired the nickname "Bottom-line Rowley."

My light felt buried in this environment, and my access to Spirit was excruciatingly spotty. I wondered where Spirit's shining Presence could possibly be seen among the gray cubicles that seemed to play a continual, low, droning song about the virtue of conformity.

Then, I met some heroes who showed me the diverse identities that Spirit can don, even within cold, black suits.

IMPERVIOUS TO THE COLLECTIVE FORCE

There were only a few men I met in the firm who operated off of a different paradigm than the firm's, the ones whose personal maps were stronger than the status quo. It was from these men that I began to learn that such a thing was possible.

One colleague was the only African-American man in the firm. We were fast friends, as we were aware that our presence represented an anomaly. Douglas taught me that work is a contract and not an obligation. He told me to be conscious about what I was trading off. He recommended that I not show up in the office on Saturdays and Sundays, as was part of the culture and my habit, especially if I was giving the firm five days and nights out of town. I considered this heretical and was fascinated by his sense of empowerment.

Levels of entitlement were built into the culture. Assistants were all women and could wear pants. By and large, they were not given much respect or attention. It seemed to me that they were treated as a means of getting client work accomplished. On the other hand, professional women, all five of us, were expected to wear suits with skirts; pants were not allowed. We were in a "higher tier."

Joe alone seemed to altogether ignore the cultural level setting. He was reliably happy and unaffected by the invisible expectations others saluted. He remained aligned with his personal map even in small gestures. One time Joe volunteered to retrieve a report Sandi, an assistant, was to have finished for our project. I saw him lean into the cubicle and stop when he saw she was on the phone.

He whispered to her, "Sandi, who are you on the phone with?"

She jumped. "Oh, I'm sorry! It's my mother. I'll get right off."

He immediately exclaimed: "No, no! Your mother is way more important than anything I have!" and he walked away without the report, still smiling. That was just his way.

My assigned mentor's name was Bob. He was a cultural misfit because he was both brilliant and funny, and he was astoundingly successful at bringing in business. When the Wall Street Journal voted him the funniest management consultant in the world, I sent him flowers and the firm subtly reprimanded him, saying they were embarrassed. Work was serious, not fun. Everyone knew that...

The business reality embraced by most people in the early to mid-eighties was reflected in a study I did for the firm, where I interviewed over twenty-five vice presidents of information systems in Fortune 100 companies. To a one, they all reported that information was the most important asset in the company.

Some of these VPs, who guarded the company's information and budding technology, reported over the head of the company's president and into the office of the chairman. Whoever had the knowledge had the power, and whoever had the technology held the company's future in his hands.

I was soon to find out that a whole new way of thinking was

emerging in the minds of pioneers whose companies would become models of future business—and, surprisingly, none of these models emerged because of technology, the global economy, world travel, or more lenient government regulation for entrepreneurs!

NIGHTMARES AND NEW MAPS

After I graduated from Northwestern, the firm granted me my request for a six-week, unpaid sabbatical. It took me four-and-a-half weeks to take my watch off while I slept. I always kept it on in case I woke up in a fog and had to figure out the time zone or date so I could be on time to catch a very early flight.

After three weeks of my break, something unexpected arose from the silence and the break of routine. I began to have horrendous nightmares of women in dungeons, screaming to be released.

Sometimes to-do lists and activities are so dense, we do not realize that we have grown to the point where our map of reality is too tight to include all that is emerging within us. If the energy of the culture around us reinforces that a tight fit is "normal," it is hard to identify stress as a signal. Then our unconscious mind helps us, sometimes finding its way to the surface and capturing our attention through dreams. Nightmares can be special messages referring us to a frazzled edge of the map of reality we take for granted.

My nightmares perfectly depicted my feminine energy—the part that operated out of compassion, interrelatedness, and the heart. I had locked away that part so I could survive in a "man's world." As I visited friends around the country and observed that not every life was as intense as the one I had chosen, I grew more exhausted.

It was the first time I felt separate enough to identify the impact of the firm's Collective Force, and that it was not in line with my energy. Through this disturbing discomfort, I began to think about how to formulate a new, more self-honoring boundary at work.

I realized that while the intellectual part of me was thriving, there were other parts of me that were completely stifled by the environment. This imbalance somehow had to be addressed. If I continued to work in this Collective Force in the same way, I knew that eventually the imbalance would reach beyond my nightmares and grab my attention through ill health.

I felt something new beginning to awaken within, and it made me very hungry to know what it was. Perhaps, with more space, I could become clearer about my best next steps. So at five weeks into my six-week sabbatical, I gathered all my courage and called my manager to ask for two more weeks of vacation.

I was not only refused, but the firm paid for an early return the following day so I could fly to my next engagement in New Jersey.

AT&T was divesting. I was assigned to be part of a team that would support AT&T in deciding how to strategically break apart the beautifully integrated, intact information systems to respond to the divestiture order. Defining my personal next steps would have to wait. However, this three-month plunge into an historic marketplace moment was to be my last consulting assignment with the firm.

DEFINING NEW TERRITORIES

As I began my new engagement, I found I had brought with me a touchstone of the impact of my nightmares. I would get severe stomach pains whenever I donned the corporate costume of a suit. Dresses became my trademark, as the feminine within me gained new authority. I was now expressing and respecting this recently emerged part, despite its opposition to the Collective Force of my firm.

As the only woman on the team, I expected comment and perhaps even rebuff on my professional garb, but instead I found the same response as when I left my high school chapel to belatedly enter my classroom. No one noticed, and no one mentioned it.

As thousands of consultants swarmed AT&T like bees to pollen-bearing flowers, I was steeped in the most exciting learning experience of my professional life. AT&T needed a new map of reality, and no one—no one on the planet—knew what that meant or how to define or create it.

One day I was in a boardroom where top managers were thinking through how to define and price new product offerings. The meeting was interrupted by an urgent request. Another high-level manager leaned into the room and said, "This (large customer) just read in the *Wall Street Journal* that we were offering (X product). He wants to buy it. What are we charging for it?"

Everyone looked at each other blankly. After a few moments of awkward silence, one manager asked, "Who told them?" Another manager mused quietly, "How did *that* get in the Journal?" After a few shrugs, a vice president said definitively, "We're selling that for four million dollars." I was sure I saw that number shoot right out of his hip. Everyone just looked wide-eyed and there was no further comment.

And that was the way some important strategic decisions were made. We were right on the edge of business imagination seeking its ground. Mapping a new business reality sometimes meant throwing a ball into a new field, lugging whatever old equipment and rules you had to wherever the ball landed, and then defining a new game around it. Boundaries would have to be defined and forged as the game evolved.

And that was the way some important strategic decisions were made. We were right on the edge of business imagination seeking its ground. Mapping a new business reality sometimes meant throwing the dart at the wall, letting it hit wherever it landed, and then working around it.

REFLECTION

Having moved from the awareness of Oneness to a fragmented reality that was confusing and chaotic, I noticed that the larger map of business was moving right along with me.

It was unprecedented that Ma Bell—the one to and from which all communication flowed— would be ordered to give power to her children Bells. She would have to trust that they would grow in knowledge and authority so that they could carry out their new power with enough good sense to survive and serve.

Just as I had no idea how to relate to the world when the One was no longer accessible to me, I saw baby Bells and Ma Bell in crisis and chaos, grasping at the scraps of what was being dismantled. They struggled to imagine how to create this new form of communication in a changing world. I noticed the similarities between my inner and outer worlds and remembered the ancient adage, "As above, so below; as within, so without."

CHAPTER FOUR

Dreaming of a Whole New World

Since I worked at AT&T five days a week, I stayed in New Jersey some weekends. At one point, I decided to attend a weekend conference called "A Tent Show: the Future of Business" at Tarrytown Conference Center. Bob Schwartz, former editor of *Time* and *Life* magazines partnered with legendary cultural anthropologist Margaret Mead to co-found the Tarrytown Group. Their mission was to "bring together feisty, leading-edge thinkers…to increase the quality of the dialogue in society."

Budding business giants sat side-by-side on a panel that actively engaged the audience in dialogue about new concepts. It was the marketplace's first exposure to the notion of finding data for decision making by listening carefully to customers and workers at all levels of the organization. The high-vibrating, exciting philosophies ignited all-new possibilities that dwarfed the gray, cubicle-built companies I had come to know in many different industries.

"In the future, we will work across disciplines, across businesses, across the world," said one panelist.

"The earth will become our business partner," declared another provocateur.

This was heretical and nearly nonsensical in an era where business bowed to individual "stars" whose status was defined by how many deals they could close and how much they could enrich the company's bottom line.

I found myself shaking. I didn't know why. My body buzzed nonstop, and I had to run around the block several times just as when I first felt Shirley MacLaine's energy on television. The future I would have most wanted if I knew what to wish for had finally arrived. This newly emerging Collective Force allowed ideas, people and resources to move like a Rubik's Cube, meaningfully interconnected and no longer fastened to a few men at the top.

The more I listened to these pioneers, the more I felt the power of new thinking popping like fireworks. In the current business reality, even the best leaders could only show up as benevolent dictators or great organizational dads. Other leaders, who paid no attention to their inner light or to their coworkers' well-being, seemed to have the power to dim the enthusiasm and creativity of an entire company under their leadership.

And then there was this new energy. It seemed to trust people's intelligence and express patience and respect when intelligence was not forthcoming. This energy also seemed to believe that everyone had something relevant to offer.

Where would these new thoughts land in the global village? I wondered if it was always true that when a group was gathered around a topic and given permission to speak its diverse mind and heart, the energy always got brighter, bigger, and more palpable. I didn't understand exactly what I was experiencing; I only knew that I wanted these values to be a Collective Force in my life. Each person was uniquely important, and the whole audience became brighter, which reminded me of the intimate interconnectedness I felt in the Light.

The tent show so fascinated me that I decided then and there to quit management consulting. I wanted to found a Center for Advanced Thinking for Young Professionals in Chicago, so that I could host speakers such as these and bring new ideas to the marketplace.

To support this dream, and while I was still consulting at AT&T, I decided to attend a two-weekend School for Entrepreneurs—a new notion at the time—also offered at Tarrytown Conference Center.

After I completed the program, Bob Schwartz asked me to consider heading up his program rather than starting my new venture. He had brought together some of the most innovative and successful CEOs in the country as models of high-integrity business. This group wanted to learn from each other and participate in each other's projects. He asked me to be the new executive director.

I thanked him, and rather than consider the extraordinary opportunity being offered, I immediately told him I was really more interested in my own business plan.

He was persistent.

Before I awoke the next morning, on the feast day of Saint Teresa of Avila, I had a dream that the conference center was filled with mirrors. In the dream I said, "This is the biggest reflection of myself I've ever seen." Then, I walked into the conference center restaurant, and after everyone had finished eating and left, I emptied the leftover scraps of desserts from the plates into a bag. I walked out with the bag slung over my shoulder. I wondered about the relevance of this opportunity at Tarrytown for my spiritual life.

I decided to be completely transparent and tell the chairman about my dream. I confessed, "It looks like I might come in, take the good stuff, and move on. In addition, you're the one with this idea. I can't have your baby, and I'm not even sure I can midwife yours to your satisfaction." He smiled, and still extended the offer.

So I quit my consulting position, and with the help of my colleague, Douglas, I drew up a contract, and we signed it.

The role turned out to involve a methodology for which I was not prepared. I realized a few years later that the chairman wanted someone who could facilitate group dynamics and participation—a role called "process consultant." This role requires skills I would not learn for a few more years. My consulting experience up to that point had trained me as an "expert consultant," which means I collected data and analyzed results to determine the best direction for clients. As the days wore on, I could sense that whatever I presented to Mr. Schwartz was not meeting with approval, yet I was without constructive feedback to learn.

Fortunately, I had good interviewing and persuasion skills and found some extraordinary leaders to add to the Tarrytown 100. Already outstanding members included Bill Gore, founder of Gore-Tex; Laurel Birch, founder of Laurel Birch Artworks, who was among the first women allowed to do business in China; and Carl Hodges, founding director of the University of Arizona's Environmental Research Lab, who helped design the Land Pavilion at Walt Disney World's EPCOT Center. They, along with other members, embraced a model of business predicated on the belief that people, not information, were the most important ingredient to business success.

This was in sharp contrast to the study I'd completed only three months earlier at the consulting firm that consistently showed Fortune 100 CEOs valued information and technology far more that the human element. The Tarrytown 100 represented a whole new Collective Force.

The first meeting of the 100 was far from stellar, and I was exhausted trying to figure out the chairman's expectations and how to meet them. He asked me to leave shortly thereafter, which I considered a blessing. In the end, my dream became reality. When I left my relatively short time there, I possessed invaluable learning and a small amount of severance pay based on the contract we had signed.

In addition to my work with business giants of the Tarrytown 100, Mr. Schwartz generously included me in his frequent cocktail parties to which he invited those he called "planetary treasures." Among the guests were some of the greatest minds and founding members of the human potential and New Age movement—about whom I knew nothing before my employment there. The chairman was a personal friend of philosophers and authors: Jean Houston, Marilyn Ferguson, Gay Luce Booth, Virginia Satir, and others.

Among other ideas, these women and their work introduced me to the notion that the body and mind are intimately connected. Up until that point, my body seemed a dense, temporary necessity, of which I would be relieved upon going Home. Through conversations and some workshops, I slowly began to explore the idea that the body has a role in accessing inner truth. I was perplexed and fascinated.

These women were not explorers of a new phenomenon. Instead, they proved to be boots-on-the-ground facilitators and weavers—of one reality into another. They seemed to use their extraordinary understanding of energy like a palate of paint, knowing that it could cause not only new ideas but also break through to new ways of thinking and being.

I felt like I had just bought a new thousand-piece puzzle and thrown all the pieces on the floor. I was just beginning to sort them out. While this was progress from my post-college years when I did not know there was a puzzle to be found, I still had no picture on the box or organizing principle to make sense of the whole. Since I was still arm-in-arm with my Dark Night guidance, life continued to operate in an area called "I have no idea what this means."

A SPECIAL KIND OF CRAZY

Shortly after returning from Tarrytown, I was on a date. Walking back to Bob's car, on a street lined with some of the most beautiful homes near Chicago's Gold Coast, I started joking. I wandered close to one of the mansions we were passing and said, "Now this manor works for me. Did I tell you my birthday is just around the corner?"

Just as I said this, a short, hooded man came out from behind a bush right in front of the mansion and pointed a gun at my stomach. He was about two feet away.

"Give me your purse!" he demanded in a loud whisper.

It was very dark, and Bob did not see the gun. He yelled, "No way.

Run!" and pushed me into the street. I tripped over his foot and heard the rip in my pantsuit as I fell and slid spread-eagle, face-down on the ground.

I waited for the gunman to pull the trigger and send the bullet through my back. In this endlessly quick moment, I felt sure I would die.

Suddenly, there was a noise. It grew louder. There were voices. A small group of friends appeared from around the corner and scared the man with the gun, who chose to run rather than shoot. His split-second and seemingly random decision allowed me the rest of my life.

As Bob helped me up from the street, all I could say was, "I'm fine. Everything is just fine. I'm fine. I just need to go home now. Yes, that's all I need. I just need to go home. Everything is fine." I said that over and over and over. I assured Bob I would be fine alone in my apartment that night. I did not stop shaking for hours on end.

I began to hallucinate, watching dark and light images merge and then separate, and kept falling into a trance-like state, chanting phrases that made no sense. In the morning, I called my friend, Lynn, and calmly asked her how she was and what she was up to that day. We chatted a while, and finally, in response to her questions about what was going on with me, I casually said, "The weirdest thing happened last night." I slowly described the incident and my nighttime state of mind as though I were relating notes from a boring lecture.

Lynn said, "Therese, you are in shock. You have to see a therapist."

"Ha!" I laughed. "I'm fine! I'm not crazy!"—which was, at that time, the basic criteria for seeing a therapist.

"You have to go to a therapist, Therese."

"Oh, Lynn, everything's fine. I guess last night was just the jitters."

Lynn was unrelenting and gave me contact information for her therapist. I did not promise to follow up, only that I would think about it.

"What would be the harm in just talking to this lady?" I asked myself throughout the day, though at the same time I could not fathom that she could be of any help…because "everything was fine."

The next night I called Lynn's therapist. As I halfheartedly told her my story, I was thinking about how glad I was that I could tell Lynn that I'd followed her advice and that her therapist was uninterested. Dr. Randall asked me about my background and seemed especially interested in my spiritual path. Then she said, "Tell me again about the details of your nighttime experience." I repeated, perhaps adding some elements as it came to me on the second round.

After listening intently, rather than scheduling an appointment, Dr. Randall said, "Therese, given your spiritual background and what you experienced last night, I'm going to give you the name of someone, and I want you to tell her I sent you. Tell her that I said she should have lunch with you, and then tell her what you just told me." I was dumbfounded.

"Who is this person?" I asked.

"She's my therapist," replied Dr. Randall.

"Ah! I must be a bad case of crazy!" I thought. "I'm going to Lynn's therapist's therapist. It's just like me to skip the basics and go right to the top!" I was really concerned about what Dr. Randall could be thinking of me.

"That's all," she ended. "Call her and go to lunch." So I did.

Dr. Powell was an attractive woman in her early forties, and she asked me several questions about my spiritual path. I did not reveal much, as I was unsure where this was headed, and based on where I was in my Dark Night, I could not discern her motives.

"Well," Dr. Powell finally began, "you and I were sisters in a past life. You are psychic. You know about magic and mysticism from past lives."

"Great! OK! Thanks!" I quickly replied. "I've got to go now." I couldn't understand how two people who seemed to think well of me would refer me to this obviously unbalanced woman. I was completely baffled and upset that I had said anything to Lynn about my date experience. I did not believe in past lives and knew nothing about psychic phenomena.

Then Dr. Powell began to tell me the content of my prayers and the saints through whom I regularly prayed at Mass! No one knew this intimate information but me—of that I was entirely certain. I could not speak.

The good doctor continued, encouraging me to go to a program founded by Warner Erhard called "EST," which I flatly refused on the basis of the cult-like method I'd heard about in this and a few other new, like-minded programs.

"Look, I have known perfectly sane people who returned from similar programs. They look glazed over and out of it, spouting some nonsense. As I understand it, they have to be deprogrammed to return to themselves. There's not a chance I'm interested. Thanks anyway."

I was astounded when Dr. Powell persisted. She told me the specific saints who were my guides and told me they wanted me to go. Again, she talked about the content of my prayers that no one knew but me.

I was finally worn out and thought, "I'm a pretty grounded person. This experience won't shake me or my faith. I will open my boundary just this once and see what it has to offer."

One of the Tarrytown 100 members had suggested I take a vacation in Florida and stay at her condo there. It turned out that EST was offering a program in the same area for the weekend, so I combined those opportunities.

Before flying down, my Dark Night companion gave me another dream wherein I was having a baby in Boulder, Colorado. The quality of the dream haunted me the next day and the next. I could not shake it. There was no man in the dream, and I sensed this was a metaphor. When I closed my eyes, however, I could feel the mountains around me like they were with me in that moment. I decided to book a plane ticket to go from Florida to Boulder after the seminar ended. At least I would explore the possibilities that my dream was a sign about my next steps on this continuing, unchartered journey called "my life."

Once down in Florida, and before I started the program, I contacted the "healer/massage therapist," Paul, whom the condo owner had highly recommended. In the middle of my first-ever massage, when Paul massaged my arms and hands, I started to See pictures in my mind of characters and quotes from the Bible. They unfolded as stories, and I reported them to him. It was as if I were both narrator and character in the story. The reports lasted as long as my hands and arms were being massaged, and then he stopped, and so did the stories.

Later, as he massaged my back, I Saw pictures of a backyard, a black-and-white spotted dog, a picnic table, and some specific people. I reported these, and Paul told me those were pictures from his childhood! The lessons from those "planetary treasures" at Tarrytown about the body-mind connection were becoming a visceral reality for me and no longer just an interesting idea.

Paul was calm and unaffected by my reports. He said that sometimes energies blend and not to let these pictures shift me from inner peace, even if they were unexpected. A year later, this man became my fiancé.

EST was my first introduction to the notion that "you create your own reality." I was a stellar student, as I thoroughly thought through all their concepts and ideas and participated fully in the exercises. However, I also challenged the instructors every step of the way, particularly asking them to stop talking in "EST code."

"If EST has anything powerful to say to us, then meet us where we are, on the ground, and with uncomplicated language," I responded, rather than answering the question asked. I also rigorously objected to their regimented methodology that treated participants like children and teachers like demigods.

Much to my surprise, at the end of the program, the head instructor asked if I would teach the program. I said, "Thank you for asking, but no. I appreciate the brainwashing, as I feel freer of some of my limiting beliefs...but I'm not interested in your value system." With that, the instructor turned his back on me and refused to talk with me again.

As I said, I didn't appreciate their value system.

Their program did, however, make an impression on me. The notion of unconscious beliefs and their related influences on behavior now held a more central place on my map of reality. This was the beginning of my new understanding that identifying and releasing fear-based beliefs creates new space inside. I decided to consciously take this newfound awareness with me to my next journey, where I expected to have my metaphorical baby.

BOULDER AND BOULDER TOWARD A NEW REALITY

Five years following my encounter with Shirley MacLaine's energy in the television, I showed up in Boulder without a clue as to why I was there or what I would do. As I settled into the hotel I'd booked, I identified myself to those I met as a management consultant. Within a few days of landing, I unexpectedly ran into a former fellow student from Tarrytown's School for Entrepreneurs. I instinctively knew that he was meant to play a role in my move to this new geography. He happened to be opening an executive conference center in a town in the hills above Boulder. After a conversation wherein I asked questions regarding his business plans, he subsequently hired me to support his strategic and operating plans to accelerate his progress on opening the center. Within a week, I was permanently relocated to Boulder.

While I was consulting, grace, wrapped in synchronicity brought me to places where leading-edge concepts and practices were beginning to emerge. This was the time in which science and spirituality began dating: world religions quietly "outed" their long-kept secrets and initiated conversations with each other; disease and illness started a relationship with mindset and feelings; predictions, prophesies, and science first shouted their oddly compatible messages; and the New Age compelled both media attention and unlikely students. New territory was being charted regularly, and a call for new maps began in earnest. These times provided some material for the reconstruction of our evolving understanding of what it is to be human—and gave me access to those who could help me group together the pieces of the puzzle on my emerging map of reality.

AUTHORING 2012

Settling into a small house near the center of town, I was anxious to take advantage of the pioneering research that was emerging from Boulder residents. One of my first encounters with leading-edge thinkers came unexpectedly through a neighbor named Jose Arguelles. Jose was an extraordinary artist and has since become known for founding the Harmonic Convergence, First Earth Days, and for announcing 2012 as a significant year for our species.

In 1953, at the age of fourteen, Jose had a luminous moment while meditating at the Pyramid of the Sun in Teotihuacan, Mexico. From that moment forward, he pursued a lifelong investigation of the mathematics and the prophecies associated with the Mayan calendar. The Mayans are an ancient civilization that developed a calendar that began in 3113 BCE and ends in 2012 CE. The Mayans called this time span "the Great Cycle."

In 1984, when I visited with Jose, he said he had been having headaches. He was up at all hours of the night "downloading" information regarding how: particular the "lay lines" that are related to longitudinal lines on the earth; human DNA; the Chinese I Ch'ing; and the Mayan calendar converged in a mathematical calculation that predicted the next planetary shift! He called the closing of the Mayan Great Cycle "the end of the book of life and the beginning of the book of love" and told me it would occur in 2012.

He was understandably excited as he showed me the letters he'd received from renowned mathematicians letting him know his theory was mathematically provable. "I'm an artist!" Jose exclaimed, shaking his head. I attended informal gatherings where Jose presented his data and findings from his first book, *Earth Ascending: An Illustrated Treatise on Law Governing Whole Systems.* It was entirely over my head, but I enjoyed the intellectual stretch.

When I asked Jose to explain more about the meaning of "lay lines," he said that different places on the planet have distinct energy fields that invite us to experience diverse aspects of life. He said Boulder was on a lay line, one of Earth's longitudinal lines that contain vortexes that compel inward reflection. I thought about the idea of the Earth itself having different levels of influences on our thoughts and behaviors depending upon the location. It was true that in Boulder, even as I continued to consult at the conference center, I also felt an unusually strong urge to "navel gaze," or focus inwardly. Jose said the strength of this energy could also cause physical sensations in the body. I was grateful for this perspective because I was about to begin my own relationship with the energy vortex of Boulder.

On a perfectly beautiful afternoon when I was hiking in the foothills, my body began to shake and vibrate. Then, I suddenly spewed words and sentences formed. I retrieved my notebook and began writing nonstop. This process happened much like the Shirley MacLaine incident—a flow of words over which my ego had no authority to control.

I was writing as though another author had hold of my hands, and I was observing the information as it was revealed. The writing predicted changes that were on their way for the planet. In addition, I found myself writing a few notes about and for the benefit of specific individuals. Incidences of spontaneous writing began to happen more often on hiking expeditions. While the information proved accurate for those that could confirm it, these episodes scared me.

I felt helpless to understand what was happening to me. I did not know if this involuntary expression was "right" or "wrong." Were these mystic gifts, or were they "psychic," as other people referred to them? Was psychic bad? Were the two the same with different names? Without the benefit of a spiritual context, I wasn't sure what they meant or if it was a "good" or "bad" thing that they were occurring. Worse than that, regardless of how I felt about it, I seemed not to be able to stop them.

At one point I took a vacation overseas. On the return flight, I met a man whom I felt was sent to me to help me know the importance of these kinds of occurrences and other things that I could not yet understand.

REFLECTION

The Dark Night led me to an unparalleled education about what was to be a new era in human history. I had a sense that, based on the unfolding changes, each person's spirit would be asked to take up its personal map and walk into the unknown. Certainly top-down authority would never again be honored in the same way. In addition, without an authority in charge, those who had a right to cry "victim" had less basis.

The idea proffered in this New Age—that we are responsible for co-creating our reality—offered fresh possibilities that challenged my imagination. As I pondered these things and felt ever excited about new visions of the future, it also felt frightening—because now there was no spiritual map I could access upon which to plot my steps to assure I was on the right track with my Maker. Was it OK to explore the new land? Would I be led astray?

CHAPTER FIVE

The Cost of Staying in "I Know"

Having had a great time visiting a friend of mine who lived in Europe, I was dreamily watching the billowy clouds out the window of the plane. Now halfway through the return flight to Boulder, I decided to stand up to stretch my legs. As I walked back to the galley at the rear of the plane, I felt an unusual urge to strike up a conversation with a gentleman who had just refreshed his drink. I remember he was wearing a golf shirt and seemed a decade or so older than me. He introduced himself as "Richard" and appeared to be very well educated by his manner of speaking. As we started chatting, he turned the conversation to details about his golf game. Although I grew bored rather quickly, having no interest in golf, I remember feeling a reserve of patience that kept me uncharacteristically lingering.

Richard turned the conversation to me and asked what I did for a living. I told him that I was a business consultant. He told me that he worked for the government and proceeded to share a few stories of his encounters and experiences with foreign heads of state and dignitaries.

Then he hesitated, and just before he began the next story, he laughed. It wasn't the self-congratulatory laugh I would have expected from a man who had been so intimate with a US president and foreign leaders. Instead, it was a self-dismissive laugh, accompanied by a sidelong glance at me. It's quite amazing how much can be revealed in a small gesture. In his laugh, I felt both his hesitation and his desire to speak about something very personal to him. I moved into a space of silence and conscious acceptance of what he might say. Perhaps he sensed that.

He slowly began to share that when working his government job, he started having dreams about what certain Middle Eastern heads of state were going to do or say in discussions and negotiations. He related stories of how, on some occasions, his dreams were so vivid that he felt as if he were actually in the offices of those dignitaries, influencing them on globally important decisions. He laughed dismissively again. I waited, hoping he would sense that I was without judgment.

After a long pause, he continued, "Then later, on my first actual visit, I knew where to go and what to say because of the events in my dreams. It was amazing, because those leaders eventually followed my recommendations point for point, exactly as they had in my dreams."

Richard gave me another sideways glance, and I nodded casually, as if he were giving me tips on which golf club to use in a sand trap. He continued, "My dreams and waking life began to interchange, and I became quite influential, and my work was very effective. I knew I was impacting important historical events and decisions. The whole time, I felt nervous and uncertain about these dreams; but the results were unmistakable.

"When my commanding officer began asking questions about these unexpected, quick successes, I reluctantly admitted where I was getting my information from and how I was following the sequences in my dreams. Since my work was top secret, I only told my commanding officer and my wife about these experiences. And even though he knew I was realizing great success, he was really spooked by the whole thing."

Richard stopped his story here and seemed to expect some excuse from me to leave. Apparently, he thought disclosing his secret would attract disapproval or avoidance, or that I might be as spooked as his boss. To support him, I simply said, "That's interesting. Yes, I've heard about these kinds of dreams. Tell me more."

His eyes grew bigger, and there was a small glimmer of hope, as if he were opening to a new possibility that would free him from his obviously self-condemning judgments. "You have experience with these kinds of things?" he asked, trying not to betray the slight optimism in his voice.

"Yes, I have had a lot of unusual experiences, and in fact, I work with people who have met with extraordinary phenomenon. And yours," I smiled and said as gently as I could, "is a mild case."

He let out a visible sigh and relaxed into a deep breath of relief and release. It was as if Richard had not exhaled since his whole dream/work coincidence began. I thought that was the end of his story and wanted to share some insights, but what he told me next almost knocked the breath out of me!

Richard said that, despite his continued and unprecedented successes, his commanding officer insisted he get mental help. The officer and Richard's wife thought it best that Richard admit himself into a mental hospital, which he did. For three months, he submitted to electric-shock treatments to try to erase the dream/reality experiences. He was also persuaded to take medication to alleviate his "mental disturbances." Upon his release he took a less stressful job and has since walked around with his head down, a bit fearful of reoccurrences. No wonder he was so shy about revealing his experiences!

The people who most loved Richard interpreted his lucid dreaming as unsafe and potentially harmful. In their efforts to keep him inside a map of reality they understood, they turned to hospitalization and medication in hopes of making his experiences go away.

Although a part of Richard may have been pulled to explore the territory behind the door of "awareness through dreams," the less intuitive part of him strongly doubted his experience. That doubt, combined with the opinions of those closest to him, became the critical mass of agreement that informed the choice he made to enter the hospital.

When people we love and trust do not have a map of reality that is wide enough to fit our experiences, they often feel afraid for us. In their efforts to limit perceived harm, they end up instead limiting and inhibiting our personal growth.

As Richard talked about the nature of what had happened to him, I subtly offered references from another perspective—references that might support him by adding an alternate view of reality. For example, I suggested that his experiences were related to natural brain and spiritual development. In addition, I offered him information on lucid dreaming and other disciplines, such as transpersonal psychology, whose academic theory and research provide a basis for understanding this kind of phenomenon.

While Richard later expressed that my perspective proved helpful, I could see that what was more important to him was that he had found a safe place to tell his story without judgment or evaluation. By relating his story to me, he'd found someone who had an internal map broad enough to include his experiences.

As we headed back to our seats for landing, Richard told me that our conversation had changed his life and that he had never felt so free. I saw that he could finally release the tightly held boundaries of his map and open to the possibility that the Universe was a friendly place and that life was provoking him toward a search for greater wholeness.

It took the power of medication to erase Richard's fearful feelings of the unknown, and help him cling to a sense of safety inside the familiar walls of his beliefs. It took a broader map of reality to ultimately free him from his fear.

As I buckled my seatbelt, I said a prayer of deep gratitude that I was not in touch with those who would have diagnosed and "treated" me according to a model that seems to have a pill for any experience beyond the map of "normalcy." I knew for certain that my energetic experiences would easily have been labeled pathological, disordered, or neurologically suspicious from the traditional medical model.

Richard taught me that when an experience lands in a territory called "I don't know what I don't know," it is a vulnerable place. It is hard to know where to focus our attention. Which assessments are credible and appropriate to help decide which direction is best? Those who love us best may be the very ones who worry that we have gone too far and, for our own sakes, want to reel us back onto the old map. Feelings of fragility follow because even if courage leads the way, we have no internal map to show us which new "neighborhoods" are dangerous and which are safe. Self-trust becomes difficult.

Yet, Richard's tale convinced me that I could not learn life's new lessons if I clung to the "I know" position in which I felt safer. Indeed, my clinging might cost me more dearly than the vulnerability and mistakes made in the unchartered course toward an unknown future.

I decided that groping in the dark in anxious confusion is as legitimate a way to learn as sitting straight and listening intently to a teacher who seems to have all the answers.

"I-don't-know," I thought to myself, "is the richest land for learning, as it compels an open mind and heart to find what may fulfill an unspoken and unknown desire."

A MEASURE OF GRACE

As I learned more about New Age concepts, they were often antithetical to my Catholic upbringing in addition to my own sensibilities. Sometimes I recoiled at my perception that people were worshiping their gifts or themselves, rather than the Author of the gifts. Gifts of healing were boldly marketed and sold as though the person possessing them were special.

It was appalling to me that outcomes were being measured. From the mystic paradigm of my youth, and even though I couldn't access my Guide, I still believed that how Spirit decides to partner with us in any situation is not our business. In fact, when I was young, Spirit would prompt me thus: "Go tell that man" (whom I did not know) "that what he just said was important." And I would. When that man cried, I would not know why, nor presume to understand Spirit's business with him. When I ask to be a companion of Spirit—to be a temple for others' highest good—I am sometimes given that honor. Full stop.

How can we measure the role we play in others' lives? Why should we think that it is our privilege to know? Perhaps I have a great gift; yet its only purpose in one instance is to plant a seed that will not be harvested until the moment of someone's death. Or perhaps simply showing up itself reminds another of someone they can suddenly forgive—while I think I'm gifting people by how my performance all comes together on stage that day!

I actually felt ashamed for the self-proclaimed saints and gurus who presumed that their gifts made them any more spiritual or special to our Creator than a quiet janitor who faithfully did his work and was good to others. The entire consciousness baffled me and felt like snake oil.

Then there were others who seemed to have pure heart and intentions. There were sincere seekers who were craving to understand, just as I was, the truth about a map of reality that had begun making its unchartered territory known. There were those whose research became the foundation for natural ways to heal the body and mind. There were those whose paths led them to unfamiliar ground and who, by their sheer focus in the service of goodwill, forged new paths for those who came after them.

I knew that in order to understand and develop whatever "gifts" were occurring within me, I had to be brave. While I still maintained my practice of going often to weekday Mass, I had to go outside the beliefs contained in the Catholic map of reality because that map was insufficient to address my current experience. Instead of open arms to consider how Spirit was currently working through my life, I found judgment and dismissal for my experiences—which are not qualities that further education and evolution in Spirit.

I knew that learning and spiritual evolution were more important to me than assuring I was in line with a set of rules and guidelines for being faithful to dogma. I believe courage is required to face the truth of what is happening within. Once the truth for us is clear, then we need to cultivate the appreciative inquiry, patience, and faith it takes to continually ask, "How can I remain in the truth of Spirit and Love, and use what is happening to serve the highest good?"

I believe that Spirit does not stop being part of my experience just because I cannot understand it or do not like it. Spirit lives inside the Dark Night.

Indeed, how can we offer future generations more value than what history has bequeathed us if we do not choose to embrace and face whatever life is bringing us now? I believe that fear stops the unfolding richness of Love—which is ultimately ever expansive.

FINALLY, A NORMAL PSYCHIC

This was a daunting time for me. It was the first time I began to know the invisible realms without the spiritual Presence that provided a sense of grounding for my questions and confusion. I observed many spiritual seekers reaching out for help from the kind of famous pioneers I met at Tarrytown. My desire was, instead, to find those who were under the radar, who's less robust resumes kept them closer to questions than answers. That way, I felt I would have more room for learning my own way, allowing mistakes, and discovering the best direction.

So I sought out and found a few good, un-famous people who taught me new models and language that helped me understand how to make choices about the mysterious movements that occurred within me. The first was Antero Alli, a psychic Reader and teacher, and now an author of several books. I found out that "psychic" was a word used in reference to the ability to See into the future or into invisible information. "Psychic" did not have a spiritual context. It was a simply an ability.

Through classes, Antero grounded me in this esoteric area of energy. His psychic Readings calmed me rather than scared me, as I had anticipated. While he spoke of past lives, which was a belief I had yet to embrace, the healing that came out of these supposed past lives felt like a release.

For example, my college sweetheart was a continuing, long-distance friend, and I found myself missing him with an intensity that would not abate—even after years. I wondered whether we could be romantically involved again. When I asked Antero to tell me about my connection with this man, without giving him any other information, Antero's first response was: "You didn't marry him, did you?"

I merely said, "No."

He said, "Good, you weren't supposed to. You and he have been together many lifetimes, and he taught you spiritual awareness. In this lifetime, you recognize him, but he does not recognize you. He has come to live this life simply—to find goodness through working with his hands and mechanical things." My friend is a mechanical engineer. After the Reading, the strength of that bond was never as intense.

I have paid that favor forward many times. Through intuitive Readings, I offer clients stories that illustrate the quality and nature of their intimate connection with those for whom relationship feels painfully attached. As their affiliation is understood from a compassionate perspective and then realigned according to that understanding, clients report, as I did to Antero, that their intense bond is no longer a distraction.

DISSECTING SPIRITUAL ENERGY

As I studied emerging bodies of work and interacted with pioneers of research in Boulder, I began to draw lines between their ideas and sensibilities and my spiritual gifts.

Before I experienced the Dark Night, I would simply and regularly receive an imprint of a whole—a Knowing that came from my heart. I thought of these imprints as "deep insight." When offered to someone in distress, the information often shifted the way he or she perceived a current dilemma, bringing greater peace.

These clear impressions occurred to me less often in Boulder. However, on some occasions when colleagues solicited my help on personal challenges, I would receive and offer deep insight. In surprisingly consistent response, many colleagues said, "Wow, you are psychic."

Having by then gleaned that "psychic" was considered a skill and not a spiritual gift, I wanted to learn more about this distinction. I attended workshops and events to explore the many terms referring to accessing invisible information. I found that psychics appear in many forms: from palm readers with neon-signed offices to fortune-tellers to crystal-ball readers to gifted "Psychic Readers" like Antero Alli.

There was a dizzying array of psychic applications: solving crimes, locating lost objects, animal whispering, contacting the dead, telling the future, channeling other entities, diagnosing physical pain. Many times I found the people who were gifted in these areas were accurate, and I was fascinated.

As I researched and decided to become the recipient of psychic information in addition to Antero's Readings, I became perplexed. Sometimes psychics offered information about which I was already aware, or information that was incomplete, leaving me to wonder what I was supposed to do about it. Other times it was clearly erroneous.

In some cases, a psychic would say "There is someone standing next to you named Marty or Mary or Matty or Michael—someone with a name that begins with 'M'." It was as though they were victims of drive-by intuitive hits. I wanted to suggest that they be still and "stay" until the whole impression was clear.

In an effort to better understand how these psychics received the information they offered, I began to observe their body language to see if I could discern the subtleties of their approach. Were they praying? Were they hearing a voice within? Were they seeing pictures in their head? Were they working with what some called "a spiritual guide" and repeating what they heard?

Soon I began to see with my eyes and sense with my own intuition that different psychics referred to different places in their bodies when they checked in to receive their impressions. For example, I could Sense the intensity of the energy around one woman's abdomen when she offered information about a family relationship. I watched another psychic focus in his head as he talked about past lives or what was coming in the future. Others obviously left their bodies, as presences that did not resemble the energy or personality of those who left began expressing in a foreign voice.

When I thought about my experience in mystic realms, I knew that I seemed to leave my body through my uplifted heart or from the top of my head. The Light was there, in front of me and above me. When, on the other hand, I received impressions, they seemed to flow down from the crown of my head and into my heart, or sometimes directly into my heart. When I stayed in my body, I perceived from the middle of my head, through what is often called "the third eye."

In one lecture I attended, the speaker referred to the places through which we receive information as "chakras." He introduced us to the ancient Hindu map of spiritual consciousness called the "chakra system." The Sanskrit word "chakra," he said, means "spinning wheel" and is associated with seven centers of the body. I wanted to better understand this map, so I sought out authors who explained it in both simpler and fuller ways.

In her book *Wheels of Life*, Anodea Judith says that each chakra "is a center for the reception, assimilation, and expression of life-force energies," and each is almost intuitively reflective of the part of the body with which it is associated. For example, the fifth chakra is located in the throat. It contains, among other things, information about the nature and quality of our self-communication.

As I read more and more about this system, I was struck by its depth and complexity. I remembered that when I was in the Oneness as a child, I had no need to break apart my Knowing into little wheels containing discrete information. Messages were whole and complete. Now, I was considering how I would receive information when my direct access to Divine Knowing felt blocked.

After my introduction to it, the chakra system became like Cliff's Notes to the whole story, reminding me of important aspects of a message, prompting me toward the Knowing that once came fluently.

KISSING MY MAP OF REALITY GOOD-BYE

While exploring the many expressions of Spirit—which others who were not religiously or spiritually inclined called "energy"—I still pined for the felt-Presence of Christ and went to Mass regularly. One day I was walking down an unpaved mountain path by myself, and without expecting a response, I asked Christ, "When are You going to come in again?" That was my shorthand for "When are You going to enter my heart, and then take me back with You into the Light?"

Now when I think about what I was really asking, the image that comes to mind is Wendy leaving the window with Peter Pan to fly to Never-Never Land. Back then, it was pure desire, yearning for fulfillment.

Christ's unexpected response forever changed my life.

I distinctly Heard His Voice—it came swiftly and was as clear as a bell. It had been some time since that Voice graced my heart. And at first, my heart leaped at this reunion. In that fleeting moment, I thought, "It's back! The Light! My sense of Oneness! Finally, I am Home again!" With joyful anticipation I turned my face toward the sky.

Then, just as swiftly as I knew the Presence was real, I Heard words that were unlike anything I had Heard Him say before.

He said, "If you love Me, divorce Me. Stop projecting your Christedness onto Me."

I was stunned. I had never Heard the word or concept of "Christ" used in this way before, and I had no idea what He could mean by this. I asked for help to understand, and as with so many other times in my life, the silence resumed.

As I pondered what in the world this could mean, I realized that not even the word "divorce" was in my vocabulary, as none of my immediate family had chosen it. Upon greater reflection, I began to understand that He was asking me to divorce my understanding of Him—whatever image I had set up and for which I had been pining. Later, in my PhD program, I would read *The History of God* by British theologian Karen Armstrong. Through her book, my eyes were opened as I read about how God has been described and worshiped in different religions of the world and at various times in history. Most especially fascinating was how the emphasis placed on the qualities of God/Source/Allah/Buddha reflected the very qualities that a particular society and culture most valued at the time.

Unless attending a specific program about spirituality, when do we stop and think about the qualities we attribute to God or Spirit—and what nuances of our hidden projections, hopes, and fears are hiding inside of them?

Does God/Spirit grow with the added knowledge of our unfolding lives, or is Spirit forever the same and we are remembering into that eternal sameness?

When I allowed His words to echo in my heart again, I just "stayed" still to see what might emerge to inform this usual occurrence. When heretical notions occurred, it was my habit to work to respectfully discern them or to feel into the words, to find out if they originated from my inner Knowing or some other kind of influence. As I learned a little later in my journey, if messages originate from another influence than Spirit, the words do not resonate in my heart, but in my head; there is a sense of confusion, rather than congruity; there is a hollow feeling, rather than a feeling of reverence.

Growing in discernment is a little like exercise. Lifting weights or moving into yoga poses, for example, requires us to feel "the good kind of pain" or muscle stress—enough that we know it is a bit beyond our norm, but not enough that it causes unhappy pain or overstress. Growth and progress are enhanced when we find that territory right in the middle.

As I "stayed" with this very strange word, "Christedness," and asked what it meant, I Heard a quote from the New Testament: "If you heed My Word, then I will live in you and you in Me." Living in you and you in Me, I thought, referred to unity. So I began to think about what mystic Communion meant to me. In the New Age terminology, it meant "going out of body" and into the Light. It was a place where all earthly concerns—even very serious ones—seemed entirely insignificant.

In my youth, identification with Love in the Light brought me an eternal perspective and peace…until I found myself back in my body. It was always quite depressing to return to this life after a mystic experience because, even as I tried my hardest to remember it, that moment of full illumination would not last. It is much like finding a perfect vacation spot in which you have a glorious feeling and you want to keep it; or a day where you want to bottle the sweet, mild, fresh air so you can open it on a particularly cold and discouraging day. It doesn't work. So you yearn to return to that spot or that climate to have the full experience again.

I wondered if asking for mystic Communion was really asking to be taken away from daily fears and anxieties—because most times, Earth was an exquisitely painful place for me. While I knew I was sensitive to others' difficult feelings and thoughts, it wasn't until I heard about other territories on the New Age maps that I had a clearer and rational understanding of my gifts in secular terms.

New Age words described my spiritual gifts in fragmented terms. "Clairaudient" means "clear hearing," or having the power to Hear others' thoughts, words, or soul-level information; "clairvoyant" means "clear seeing," or having the power to See into the meaning of things, into the future, or to perceive stories of other lives or archetypes that have meaning for another person; and "clairsentience" means "clear feeling and sensing," or having the power to keenly and accurately Feel or Sense other people's or groups feelings. I had not yet opened to my work as a medium in communicating with those who have passed, but I had also had a few incidences of "channeling," where a voice other-than-mine expressed itself through me.

Reading about these gifts, I began to understand why, when

someone was going through a particularly difficult time, I would Sense it and keenly Feel it. Here is the key: those with clairsentience (or "clear feeling") in particular are most tuned into the denied feelings of others.

Most people only deny feelings like fear, anger, grief, and anguish. So if you have clairsentient giftedness, it means you can be Feeling someone's denied rage and perhaps the terror they feel underneath it, even as they smile at you and tell you everything is just great. What's worse is that if you ask if they are feeling what you are, because those feelings are not conscious for them, they may invalidate your intuition and even call you "crazy." In addition, without consciousness or any training, it is challenging to discern whether those feelings are someone else's or your own—because they can feel just like your own.

Because clairsentience had made my human journey emotionally precarious, perhaps Christ, while as dear to my heart as could be imagined, had also become a kind of Peter Pan in my memory. I just wanted Him to take me to Never-Never-Experience-Pain-Again Land. Perhaps He was strongly suggesting that it was time for me to grow up and to "stay" inside my body and human experience. Even if that was a great idea, let's just say it was not a happy thought for me.

It would mean building the skill to create boundaries through which I could distinguish my feelings from others'. It would mean staying in my body even when a family, community, or the world was having a horrific time of things and I could Feel that. It would mean committing to finding out what life was like in my body when I could more easily move into other, more comforting realms.

If faith led me to imitate Christ, then I had to choose to courageously and fully embrace life as it was given to me, and build trust that I would be guided through it—even in the Dark Night. I reminded myself that Jesus had clairsensory gifts and plenty more. Yet He stayed in his body to endure the pain of humiliation, rejection, torture, and death. As I further reflected, I imagined that what was even more challenging for Him was His capacity to Feel and Know the enormity of human ignorance, the fear behind greed and violence, the pain of voiceless suffering, and the personal and multi-generational, global tragedy of forgetting we are intimately part of a Source that is eternally loving.

This kind of faith gave me a different perspective about intuitive capacities, such as clairsentience and clairaudience, which was not widely shared in some of the workshops I attended. I recall how this difference played out in one instance when I was in a meditation class run by a psychic institute. At break, my fellow workshop participants and I would mingle with participants of the institute's two-year training program that certified them as clairvoyants. I glanced at a gentleman on my way to the restroom, and he smiled at me. I suddenly felt so drawn to this man that I literally stopped and stared at him. He continued to smile without saying a word.

Even though I was seriously dating someone at the time, out of the blue I began to think about how attractive this man was and how wonderful it would be to date him. Just as I started to think about how to break up with my boyfriend so I could make that image real, I shook myself out of what felt like a trance.

Anna Beth, the institute's co-founder, happened to be standing nearby. I was so upset about what happened that I told her the story.

She smiled and nodded, with a slight toss of her head in the gentleman's direction. "Yes," she confirmed, "that's him! Remember, this is a psychic institute, and some people are using their power to influence others. You'd better be more aware of your power or there's no telling what can happen."

While I was grateful to remember the importance of using personal power consciously, I realized for the first time that the institute held the belief that psychic power was not related to values. In their courses, they taught that participants had free will to use their psychic power in whatever way they chose. While that is obviously true, there was no conversation in any classes about the ethics of using this hidden influence solely for one's own gain, or for the overt manipulation of another person's will. Neither could one find dialogue about the spiritual, moral, or even karmic consequences of doing so.

I believed then, as I do now, that values are inherent in every decision we make—whether or not we are aware of it. I learned both privately and in working with corporations that it is enormously important to explicitly discuss what values are at play in relationships and choices. Without revealing them, values become hidden assumptions woven into communication, making common ground harder to find. After this experience at the institute, I began to include values and intent as important parts of conversations about the inner workings of our psyches.

Despite the fact that I could not touch into the nurturing Light as I had known it before the Dark Night, I wanted to use gifts of Seeing, Hearing, Feeling, and Sensing the hidden realms to help souls be at peace. I wanted to remind myself and others that we belong to a Love that is ever-present, though not always consciously available.

I learned that we have a choice about how we relate to and use our hidden power—including the choice to pretend that our intent and the beliefs behind it don't matter. Somehow, on this road less traveled, I would live and teach intuition in a way that honored our power to love.

I began to notice and question the intention of each intuitive practitioner I met, and how values influenced the method used as well as the outcome. When the practitioner's intention was to "heal the broken," for example, I felt less comfortable than when she was "helping a client remember that he is already whole."

In reflecting on my beliefs, intentions, and values, I concluded: I am a spiritually committed person, and my intent is to align purpose and essential gifts with the potential for creative contribution in the world. While others who experienced my gifts at that time referred to me as "psychic," I thought of myself as "a mystic with psychic symptoms."

During this process of groping in the dark to find my spiritual center, a friend gave me two quotes from twelfth-century Christian mystic Meister Eckhart, which I took to heart and which helped remind me of the new path to which I was about to commit:

"The ultimate and highest leave-taking is leaving God for GOD, leaving your notion of God for an experience of God which transcends all notions."

"The knower and the known are one. Simple people imagine that they should see God as if he stood there and they here. This is not so. God and I, we are one."

Again and again throughout the years, I have returned to these quotes to guide me in times when I felt satisfied that I understood Christ, Spirit, Source, and/or God.

While revelation and wisdom are the fruits of dedicated labor in Spirit, what I have had the privilege of learning may be considered a speck in the sand of one of God's beaches. Along the way, my exploration has often brought me to my knees in lessons of humility—sometimes accompanied by humility's unprocessed brother, humiliation—to assure that I don't mistake my ego's idea of what is true for wisdom of a higher order that is revealed in its own time.

Rather than "projecting my Christedness" onto Christ, I sought after a way to faithfully follow His request to divorce my understanding of Him—knowing I was really asking to be introduced to a greater understanding of Him. Perhaps as we develop, we need to be in touch with the parts of our Creator that have the most meaning for our evolution in the moment. Since the unknowable God is larger than our mind's ability to understand, the best we can do is allow our map of reality to open to greater truths as our paths unfold.

The first order of business in my relationship with the unknown Christ—as in any growing, intimate relationship—was to make a specific commitment. After that, help would come to show me the way to fulfill it. And so, in an act of faith, and having as little understanding of what I was getting myself into as I did when I was six years old, I made a commitment to a new map of reality. This one would have something to do with "staying" in my body and learning what it meant to have a conscious spiritual relationship fuel my boots-on-the-ground experience.

REFLECTION

Through business and other adventures in Boulder, I learned about many territories that created new meaning for me. Among the most important was how, as humans, our perceptions, behavior, and choices are significantly influenced by unconscious, invisible energy fields, such as:

- Unconscious beliefs
- Dreams that linger and whose quality are markedly different than everyday dreaming
- Collective unconscious beliefs as a Collective Force
- Energy fields called "lay lines" of the Earth

I also began to understand that as we grow, so does our relationship and understanding of an unknowable God. Opening to what I cannot yet comprehend can enhance what is possible as a spiritually growing human.

CHAPTER SIX

Gently Accelerate That Out of My Body, Please

As I began my newly committed embodied life, I was a bit fearful about the ongoing impact of feeling others' angst. Thankfully, I found that Boulder was also a Mecca of leading-edge experiments for resolving physical, psychological, and emotional pain. Through my several years of consulting, I had been schooled in efficiency and effectiveness— how to squeeze the most value out of the smallest investment. In that spirit, I went on a personal search to find "the most accelerated method of transformation for releasing painful feelings and coming to peace."

While I fancied this an excellent research proposition, I was truly in earnest to find a path I could trust, since I could no longer distract myself with the hope of mystic rescue. Little did I know that grace had led me to the very best place to begin training to "stay" and even explore physical pain for the surprising wisdom it contained.

Over the next couple of years, I experienced dozens of modalities for releasing old patterns of belief, behaviors, feelings, and habits. Ever equipped with my pit-bull curiosity, I went full bore into the emerging field of "alternative" healing. There were "push it through" and "command it out" kinds, "physical scream" kinds, "observe and let go" kinds, "analyze and evaluate" kinds, "dance it out" kinds, "deep massage" kinds, "pray with abandon" kinds, "hook up to the brain with feedback" kinds, and "behavioral cue change" kinds. While I found value and benefit in every kind, when I evaluated the research for the most accelerated kind, what I found was completely unexpected.

Hypothesizing that I would find a method that would be described as "hard and fast, make-it-go-away" healing, which matched my consulting style and assumption about how to accelerate things, I was shocked to find something altogether different. I discovered that releasing old patterns of belief and behavior and setting conditions for new brain connections occurred most effectively and quickly through a soft, slow, subtle approach!

The prevailing paradigm in business and other institutions at the time worshiped at the altar of masculine energy—hard, fast, competitive, and often ruthless. That is the model in which I had been dunked, and which I had personally adopted to stay alive in a cutthroat environment. Qualities of "soft" and "subtle" were dismissed, devalued, and proactively subordinated in the marketplace. This alternative-healing encounter taught me about the power of feminine energy, as if the Divine Mother were inviting the human heart to grow hands to reach for the compassion of her own arms.

I was privileged to meet Ron Kurtz, PhD, who also lived in Boulder at the time. He founded a psychotherapy he called "Hakomi," a Hopi Indian word that means: "How do you relate to all these realms: Self, Other, and Great Spirit?"

Hakomi honors the body as a defining source of information about why we feel and choose to behave as we do. In this form of therapy, the client remains mindful, while the therapist offers space and time for the client to notice his or her body-specific sensations and responses to the therapist's simple word and phrase probes, such as "your needs are important."

Noting my astonishment at the skillful patience of the Hakomi therapist, and my discomfort at being gently told, "take your time," I became aware that my experience in a family of thirteen people had definitely made space my "final frontier."

A central tenet of this therapy is that the unconscious mind is a very powerful influence and organizer of our reality. Furthermore, it postulates that the sensations in the body offer significant clues as to the agenda of the unconscious. It was entirely new for me to imagine the body as a friend instead of a source of persistently painful distraction from more important matters.

Through Hakomi I learned that the body was "matter" and that it does, indeed, matter as a devoted partner to inner thoughts and feelings. Even as the Dark Night's spiritual loneliness continued, this blessing was profound. Rather than hold my nose and suffer in my body, as my narrow imagination had projected, now I might get to know my body as a willing companion on my earthly journey!

PAY ATTENTION!

It took me some time to feel sensations in my body, as I was unaccustomed to paying attention. In the current consumer environment, with more stimuli than ever imagined in human history, it is a challenge to find anyone who has the capacity and fortitude to pay attention to subtle physical sensation.

Hakomi postulates that feeling sensation is learning unto itself, and must be patiently cultivated. It is a critical skill for psychological, emotional, physical, and spiritual health. Without the capacity to recognize subtle sensation, we risk missing signals that can keep us in balance, until they show up in less and less subtle ways—and then more painful reconciliation awaits us.

Robert Masters wrote a book called *NeuroSpeak* that helps people tune into their sensation as they read. For example, "I'm feeling a tingling sensation inside the big toe of my right foot right now." As you read that sentence, the brain follows and obeys. This enhances the brain's awareness and trains your brain to remember that you are in a body and can detect minute feelings. Before I read that short, simple book, I had no idea that I had any feeling on the pad of my right foot between my smallest toe and the next one!

Other methods of healing that I studied in Boulder were cognitive in nature, assuming that the head could work things out by talking, or that symptoms could be expressed without connecting them to the belief that was behind the symptom. Still others recommended remaining silent, without guidance. Several methods moved quickly to cuddling the inner child.

In learning the principles of Hakomi, I interpreted that if there was an inner child, it was more about respectfully seeking to understand her sometimes-complex assistance. The unconscious is often like a very smart child who takes the fear to which we pay no attention and builds forts and structures that keep the fear safe inside—unassailable—so we can consciously pretend it doesn't exist. Then the forts and structures start to get in the way of other things, and produce "symptoms." However, the symptoms have something to do with forts, not the fear. That's why it's hard to get to the fear.

Hakomi believes that you can make friends with the smart kid who built the structures, admiring the strength of her construction. When appreciation is actively and sincerely offered, the smart kid relaxes to know that her work is seen and understood as helpful. Then the therapist can ask, "What's important about that fort?" And pretty soon, the inner kid spills the beans, and with gentle patience, the fear is identified.

Since that kid probably built her fort a long time ago, we likely have more resources in our current life to face the uncovered fear and release it. Even that process is done with profound respect for whatever the inner child needs—just as we respect that each person grieves differently when a loved one dies. We can never assume we understand another person's pain or what support and timing are most helpful for her to face it. After the entire structure is dismantled and the smart inner kid is relieved of her duties, there is a process that identifies and lays the foundation for more supportive and helpful beliefs.

We can only expand our capacity to know the richness of life when we say yes to what Albert Einstein posited as the most important question we can ask: "Is the Universe a friendly place?" Strength that is gentle and kind creates a sense of safety, which supports relaxation and unfolding—both of which are necessary to releasing old patterns that are stuck together for a good reason. What Hakomi is trying to accomplish, in the end, is to let all the parts of a person know that they are seen, heard, and understood.

Dr. Kurtz once told this story: "I was walking down the street on a beautiful Sunday afternoon, and out of nowhere came a very large dog wildly barking as he bounded toward me. My first reaction was to jump, yell, and run, but instead I looked the dog right in the eye and said, 'Oh! You scared me; you really scared me! Good job!' The dog suddenly stopped barking."

Dr. Kurtz said, "I wanted to let the dog know he did a good job in his intention to scare me. That's really what all of us want—to be seen for our intent; and when we are, we quickly calm down."

As deeply grateful as I was for Hakomi's profound help in partnering with my body to reach inner wisdom, and for the navel-gazing time in Boulder, I assumed I would use all I had learned for personal growth and then go back to business consulting. Becoming a therapist to accompany people week after week in ongoing therapy was not my comfort zone. Breaking new ground inside me and for organizations was my passion, so consulting was once again on my radar screen.

Just then I had another dream that made me rethink my work and its essential nature.

HAND THAT DREAM OVER TO ME

Silver Springs, Colorado, sits among trees so tall and thick with leaves that there is no use trying to see the top of them. Small orange foxes and families of deer smell the ground for food. After I had driven for a while on a dirt path, the house I was renting for a month came into view. Having finished my consulting with the conference center leader for whom I was working, I was taking a break. I shared the house with the healer I'd met in Florida, Paul, who was then my fiancé.

As a business consultant who for so long had valued a full schedule, the prospect of space and time without agenda felt a bit scary. Yet I knew that once I committed to it, silence had always been an unceasing friend to me. And recalling my six-week break from consulting, I remembered that space allows unexpected pieces of my unconscious to find their way to the surface. And again, it happened through a dream:

I was following a tall, older man in a turban through the field at the first light of dawn. I had very long, dark, thick hair and was about eighteen years old. Although I knew in the dream that this young woman didn't look like me in this life, I was also aware that I was her. We arrived at a hospital. As we entered, the very few people taking care of patients bowed toward the man ahead of me, who apparently was a doctor. He told me to lay my hands on particular patients. I did as I was told, closing my eyes, bowing my head, and feeling tingling moving from my hands into each person's head. After doing this with multiple patients, as the next shift of people began to arrive, we took our leave.

When we returned home, I saw a book on the fireplace mantle. It was in a language that had many characters. As I stared at the book, I said, "I know what this says, but I cannot remember how to read it." It seemed to be written in a language different than the one associated with my home in the dream. Still, I said in frustration, "Why can't I remember this language? I know it!" Then I woke up.

As I began to wonder what that was about, I turned over and went right back to sleep. Immediately I saw two arms that were glowing with golden light from elbow to fingertips on a black background. There was nothing else in the frame. "They are so beautiful!" I exclaimed. Then I took a sharp in-breath as I realized they were attached to my upper arms, and they were mine! I awoke.

I went downstairs and said to Paul, "You won't believe the dreams I just had! They were so vivid. Not like regular dreams. I have to tell you about them." Paul had been painting. He was taking a course on ancient Chinese calligraphy. He stopped at my excited voice.

I told him about the dream, and as I got to the part about trying to read the book on the mantle, I said, "There were characters like...like..." At that moment, my eyes nearly popped out of my head as I saw what Paul had been painting. "Like those!" I blurted out. "Those are the characters I saw in my dream! What do they mean, Paul?" He slowly traced the letters with his fingers as he said, "They mean 'healing hands.'"

As my mind swam between the weaving of my waking and sleeping lives, I remembered Richard's story. "Don't dismiss this!" I reminded myself. Paying attention then to the dream itself, I was dumbfounded. Up until this point, I could not even fathom myself as having any "healing gifts."

However, I could not ignore the vivid sensation that began to increase in my hands and arms in the days and weeks following this dream. I began to experience other things as well, such as Knowing someone had a particular physical pain by looking at them from across a room, touching someone and having them tell me they felt better in mind and body, and discerning spirits that were not those I knew from my early Catholic experience.

Before pursuing what all this could mean, I had yet another dream—this time it was pointing me in the direction of the Bay Area in California. It was followed in my waking hours by a compelling pull to go west. I knew a chapter of my life had ended.

Fortunately, Paul was well aware of my penchant for Hearing and following Spirit wherever it led. He was in Nepal at the time of my westbound dreams, so I wrote and told him to fly back to San Francisco instead of Boulder because we were moving. As was his patient and steady way, he wrote back, "OK. Sounds interesting. I'll call when I have access to a phone."

HOW FREE IS OUR WILL?

The Bay Area seemed to have more PhDs per square inch than anywhere else in the country. Most of the established business consultants seemed to more jealously guard their client base than in Chicago or Boulder, and they often charged for the privilege of networking and referral, even if it resulted in no work.

While working hard to establish my independent consulting practice, I had more down time than I'd hoped. Seeking to continue my spiritual and energetic education, I decided to take some basic meditation courses at a place called "Psychic Horizons." Just as in Boulder, in this context, "psychic" had no spiritual foundation and was purely an exercise to increase the acuity of the third eye to See into the invisible realms.

After studying the distinction between "spiritual" and "psychic" in

Boulder, I grew past my fear and criticism of all things "psychic." In sincerely pursuing development and a better understanding of the gifts that still seemed to overtake me on a regular basis, I knew that my spiritual foundation could not be shaken.

My first teacher at Psychic Horizons was another un-famous, kind, and quiet woman named Judy Tergis. Judy taught me the meaning and importance of neutrality by the way she instructed and engaged students. To this day, I have never heard Judy judge anyone or anything, always having a ready smile to meet new information.

Once during class, I began to wiggle and shift in my chair. Judy walked near me and said with curiosity, "What's going on?"

"Well," I replied, "I'm shaking again. I can sense that there is a spirit that wants to come through me, and I'm trying to ground myself."

Judy's soft smile returned. "Well, you can do that…or you could just say no."

"I can?" I cried incredulously.

"Therese, you have free will. No spirit has more authority than you do in your life—no matter how great that spirit is. You decide—and then say what you want."

I was dumbfounded. In all the times in the past few years that these surges of energy poured through me, it never occurred to me that I had any say in it!

"Wait a minute," I thought indignantly. "I have been praying and praying that if any energies coming to me or through me were not for the highest good, that Spirit would give me a sign or stop it from flowing—yet the energy went on unabated. If the energy weren't 'meant to be' for me, why wouldn't God have stopped it?" I didn't want to be out of alignment with God's will, even if I could no longer feel that strong sense of being on track or off it.

I never entertained the idea that if I prayed and felt no change, that I had the free will and the power to say "I don't want this"—and that such a stated conviction would be sufficient to influence or dictate the outcome. Throughout my childhood I had practiced unbending obedience. I assumed that if there was no change in the energy that came to me after I prayed, it must be God's will to allow it.

From the perspective of Oneness in the mystic realms, there is no free will…because clearly the contract has already been signed, the commitment made. The "yes, I will do Your will" is not up for debate or amendment, nor does it hold any other position in everyday reality but the most fundamental—it is the organizing principle of life. That contract could clearly be carried out when access to "God's will" seemed within reach. In the Dark Night, when access to that inner Knowing was denied, a new season had begun.

Slowly I began to understand that it was time to make my own decisions without the readily available Knowing. Just as with human psychological and emotional development, teens on their own for the first time come in contact with situations with which they are unfamiliar. Relying upon the values they have consciously or unconsciously integrated since childhood, they experiment.

The results allow them to intimately shape their character—not from making the right decision every time, but from the willingness to learn from the outcome of whatever choice they make. Noted psychologist C. G. Jung calls this the "individuation process." I realized that I was following this path in my spiritual development as well.

FROM ONENESS TO ONLY ONE

In learning to perceive from the perspective of my own preferences, questions of identity that never occurred to me in Oneness now seemed persistent. Who was I in this new world and with these gifts and with my own desires? Unity is a "we." Now I felt I somehow had to carve out an "I."

In C. G. Jung's individuation process, carving out the "I" or ego is the first order of business, and then upon reflection over time, wisdom moves us toward greater understanding of our connectedness with one another; finally we seek unity. I was doing it all backwards.

I began to think about the polarities of my interests—a passion for priesthood, loving the deep silence of a relationship with the Divine, and a passion for business, loving the extroverted environment and the complexity of politics seeking to align with purpose.

Instead of being led to niches within the Church where I had hoped to blend both gifts, such as the archdiocese program, my faith journey had directed me away from this channel. In fact, my dreams led me to situations wherein learning to see my spiritual gifts from other perspectives was practically unavoidable.

"There must be a reason for converging experiences from left and right, from one world to the other…but what could it possibly be?" I mused.

The "who am I in the world?" question continued as if it were an affliction to be addressed. When the vertical wonder of looking up into Oneness is out of reach, the horizontal plane is the next imperative—

where information is obtained through fellow human beings. I decided to go back to my own beginning.

"How in the world," I thought, "is there no one in my immediate family, including eighty-five or so cousins, uncles, aunts, nieces, and nephews, who possesses esoteric gifts? What about my ancestors? Did they have such gifts? If they did, were they given the opportunity or permission to identify or express them? Can my ancestry explain how my passion for business landed side-by-side with my passion for Spirit? What could have gotten into my DNA that would have juxtaposed these unlikely bedfellows?"

Sifting through the few stories that my parents related about their deceased relatives, I sought any inkling of resemblance to either side of my passions. Perhaps if I could find a role model, it would help me better understand who I was and what to do about it. When my father told me about his dad's life, I felt as though I'd found another piece to my emerging puzzle.

My dad said that my grandfather's sixth-grade education was three years more advanced than his wife's, who made it through the third grade. He was a gregarious man, with vision and an eye for moneymaking ideas that would support his growing family. At the steel mills on Chicago's South Side, he became the steel mill "barber" (substituting a smile for training) and during breaks and lunch would cut his coworkers' hair for a quarter.

One day Grandpa met a man who had invented a formula that could clean the oil and paint off a hardworking man's hands. He immediately saw a business opportunity, and was convinced this was a revolutionary product. He talked the man into letting him sell the product door-to-door. On several occasions, my grandfather asked the old man if he could be his partner in finding a way to make and sell the product for a larger audience. The old man did not understand or buy into my grandfather's vision.

My grandfather then asked him for the formula, and said he would even be happy to wait until the old man retired. But the old man refused, and he died with it safely tucked away in his own head. Within a year of the old man's death, lye soap was introduced to the market, and my frustrated grandfather knew that he could have been part of that success if only he could have convinced the old man to share his vision or give him the formula.

Grandpa next talked several friends and relatives into lending him the money to buy two apartment buildings. This was a mystery to those around him because it was a time when people thought of real estate as a way to secure a home, rather than as a moneymaking investment for the future. It may have been the perfect idea, but my grandfather did not anticipate the Depression. While he kept up the buildings, he did not have the heart to charge tenants rent when they were experiencing such hard times.

When the Depression ended and everyone readied for brighter times, people began moving away from the deteriorating neighborhood. So, my irrepressible grandfather had another idea. He thought that if neighbors would band together and work in cooperation, they could make sure all the families felt safe and that property was well maintained. This would keep his and everyone else's real estate investment safe as well.

This idea was obviously the forerunner to a neighborhood

association, though at the time no such model existed. So, my grandfather gathered his neighbors together to present and discuss his idea. My dad attended the gathering, and watched as his father stood on a short, wooden stage and struggled to find words to convince people to band together.

Grandpa stumbled and fumbled until he finally gave up, humiliated. He turned to my Dad with tears in his eyes and deep disappointment in his heart. He said, "They don't understand. They are not getting it. If I had an education, I would have the words and I could make them understand." Sadly, the neighborhood real-estate value continued to decrease until the family gave up and abandoned the buildings, never to recover Grandpa's investment.

Yet, my grandfather carried on, deciding that his children would not experience the pain of his past. His conviction about the value of education caused him to offer my father only three choices of profession: doctor, lawyer, or dentist. My father chose the one where his patients could hear his soft, kind, velvet voice close to their ears, and in their hypnotic contentedness, forget they had all manner of instruments in their mouth.

My grandfather's value of education, founded in his failed, desperate attempts to translate his vision into reality, was so etched in my father's heart that he passed Grandpa's gift on to me and to my siblings. Through many decades of my father's dedicated work, all ten of my siblings and I attended Catholic high school, all of us went to college, and many of us have advanced degrees. I am grateful to my grandfather for his response to his personal pain that, through my father's hard work, became our blessing.

At the same time—and here's where the resemblance came into greater focus—I wondered if Grandpa's challenge was perhaps less that he was missing the educated words to describe his vision than that he was attempting to describe a horizon his listeners had never known, and that had not yet emerged as a reality.

His irrepressible optimism and eye for emerging opportunities brought him face to face with a future that made sense to him because he could see how things fit together in a way his friends and neighbors could not.

Seeing how things fit together and not having the language to express that wholeness is the dilemma I have lived with since childhood. I ached at the familiarity of this struggle—even as I held the academic degrees in hand that my grandfather's struggle and response afforded me! I was grateful for this insight. I also realized that, while Grandpa's experience helped me understand my passion for entrepreneuring, it did not explain the other side of my passion.

THE MYSTIC PAST

Still curious about my mystic side, I kept looking for more clues. My brother, Gene, enjoys a hobby in genealogy and is as talented as any professional in the field. He was the catalyst for my family's learning about the fascinating study of our genetic origins. As I read his research, I also began to think about relatives even farther back than historical records allow.

According to Gene, who is also my Irish twin at ten-and-a-half months my senior, our family roots since the early 1800s are 100 percent Irish Catholic, with the exception of one English horse thief. My grandmother claimed he didn't count—not because he was a horse thief, but because he was a Protestant. Some people say that being Catholic is a lot like being Irish—it's in your blood. Even if you walk away, it sort of walks away with you. Whether it's the guilt that comes unbidden as you look down at the meat you are eating during Lent on Friday or the sense that God really does keep score, Catholic experience sticks like flypaper.

In my later years, I realized that in addition to this Catholic map that held a central place upon which to plot my mystic gifts, those gifts also resembled an earlier part of my bloodline. If you go back far enough in my family's heritage, you will find the ghosts and leprechauns that spring from the Irish forests and into our fairy tales. Then, of course, there is the rich Celtic priestess tradition, depicted in books like *The Mists of Avalon*. Ironically, it was our own Catholic saint, Saint Patrick, who drove out the priestesses after the first millennium so that mystic seers, herbal and spiritual healings, and our natural relationship with the planet became a thing of the past.

While many Irish farmers today still keep a tree in the middle of their farmland to accommodate the fairies whose earth portals are located under it, much of the folklore has been muted. I believe that Ireland's notoriety for alcoholism and self-deprecating humor may be due in large part to the fact that by religious edict they were discouraged from expressing—indeed they had to repress and depress—their colorful, spiritual nature.

This ancient Irish conflict between religion and spirituality was reflected as clearly in my childhood in the Catholic Church's prohibition on the women's power and priestly entitlements, as in the time when they crushed the Celtic priestesses' Seeing and Healing gifts. And here I was in the twenty-first century, wondering what this could all mean.

Even as I began to see that my odd confluence of paths and passions had streams that flowed from my ancestral heritage, they were still juxtaposed. How could I bring these opposing sides together and be faithful to my path? In praying for this unlikely convergence, how could I learn to trust myself? And which "self" should I trust—the one who loves business, or the one who loves healing and feels like a priest? When I allow my desires to have their way with me, how do I stay aligned with Spirit, and how can I tell my ego from Spirit?

Pondering these big questions one day, I remembered that Hakomi postulated that the body cannot lie. When there is internal conflict, the body will show it in some form. To decode the body's symptoms would be a way to tell myself the truth and a way I could learn to trust myself. What felt right? What did I want?

I'd never asked myself those questions before. So instead of using Hakomi only as a tool for dealing with overwhelming feelings from my gift of clairsentience, I would now use that tool to learn to trust myself by listening in to my body. Little did I know that this body-intelligence would also become a critical friend to me as I began my next adventure in business.

REFLECTION

For the first time in my life, I found the body to be an important partner in spiritual expression. Thinking about myself as an embodied spirit, rather than a spirit who had to put up with a body, became an unexpected identity crisis. Exploring the threads of my DNA helped me better understand ancestral influences on my disparate passions. With all this new understanding, I reentered the workforce to serve and to express my new self.

CHAPTER SEVEN

Oh No, We're Free!

Taking my body-intelligence lessons with me, I decided it was time to express myself in a new way, a way that applied my spiritual nature in a grounded or "embodied" way. For me, there is nothing more grounded in the everyday than business reality.

This time, however, rather than lose myself in the company culture as I did in the big-six consulting firm in which I'd worked a few years before, I would find a way to apply my evolving faith journey in the hallowed halls of the new marketplace.

It was a few years after Tarrytown, and their cutting-edge business models had not yet become mainstream. In fact, the marketplace was just beginning to embrace technology; competition was emerging in unlikely places, and for the first time, businesses slowly began to understand that telling people what to do was not sufficient to assure success. As is now well-known, until technology became common, people were told to leave their brains as well as their emotions at the door, and to just do their jobs. This was finally changing.

When I began consulting again, I witnessed with surprise that when workers were "liberated" and told their independent thinking would be valued, their response was far from the happy cry of those who could finally run free. It was more like the story Tobi told me in college about what happens when Jesus comes to open the jail door and we suddenly feel a strong preference for our comfortable cage.

Running free at that time was a scary prospect because most people had trained themselves to dull down their awareness, follow the rules, and make the best of things. A powerful Collective Force had defined a space of conformity where personal responsibility was discouraged. Workers could lose the support of leaders and coworkers, and even their jobs, if they went against the tide. Moving beyond this historic status quo, workers were carefully stretching their minds, still fearful of the consequences.

After several months of working with organizations in this painful stage of change, I took a break with my friend, Mary, to visit another friend, Belinda, who lived near Lake Landau in Germany. Ten days before our plane arrived there, the news reported that the Berlin Wall had come down. We were overjoyed at this "coincidental" historic opportunity!

After settling into the guestroom of Belinda's house, we worked out a plan for a side trip to East Berlin. The next day, we traveled to the border and watched the revelers, who were still in full celebration mode. I held a piece of the Wall in my hand and imagined those whose pathways had been defined by the existence and security of the Berlin Wall for the past thirty years: one country, two utterly opposite maps of reality.

We passed through the renowned Checkpoint Charlie, which was known as "the Gateway to East and West Germany," noticing banana peels all over the ground as East Berliners ate fresh fruit for the first time in decades.

As currency was exchanged so we could purchase East Berlin products and services, my excitement grew, imagining the happy faces of those who had recently been liberated. Mary and I had every expectation that the jubilation we witnessed at the Wall would be visible everywhere.

As we walked through the historic square where the twelfth-century government buildings were clustered, it was almost deserted. In fact, there was a gray pallor that seemed to hang in the air, and I had a feeling of foreboding. Walking farther into town, we noticed the pale faces on many very thin people who walked with their heads down. Mary and I exchanged surprised glances and decided to keep wandering.

Walking through the half-open door of a store, the first thing we noticed, directly at eye level, were very skinny, dead chickens with little meat on them, hanging pathetically from the string around their webbed feet.

On the table under the chickens were glass jars containing vegetables (I think), smashed down, as if they were desperately signaling for rescue. Nearby, there were loaves of bread, without any wrapping covering them, strewn across a long, white plastic table.

Wide-eyed, Mary and I decided to go to another part of the store. We saw a set of three black gloves, laid side-by-side in a glass display case. We wondered about their uniqueness and high value. As we peered closely into the case, we realized that these were vinyl gloves that would likely sell for two or three dollars at Kmart. They were on sale for what translated to about thirty US dollars.

Suddenly we heard loud German shouts and looked up to see the one saleswoman behind the case frowning at us and shaking her head. She pointed to the side of us, and we saw a line of fifteen or so women waiting to view the gloves—and perhaps try them on—one person at a time, like they were touching the crown jewels. Mary and I exchanged a shocked look and apologized in the best German we could muster as we hurried out of the store.

In a nearby soda shop, we thought we would finally find the celebration that seemed absent from the rest of our wandering tour. As we walked in, a person behind a small concession stand had on display nylons, cigarettes, and a sign for the two flavors of ice cream they offered. Suffice it to say the ice cream was unlike any we had tasted.

There were people in the shop sitting at two person tables, silently smoking as they looked past each other. No one was smiling. To keep in line with the atmosphere, we whispered, occasionally looking around to see the glances of people who detected strangers. I noticed a calendar on the wall. The large picture opposite the grid of days and weeks was a painting in gray and black that closely resembled artist Edvard Munch's "The Scream."

Back in town, I Felt into the energy that permeated the town square. The picture that came to me was sewer covers lying on the ground, revealing something bubbling beneath the surface of the streets that had yet to emerge…and surely it would not be a happy flow.

I began to wonder, "In places like this, where individual expression is devalued and discouraged, what happens to imagination? What happens to the capacity for creativity or even to feel into the sensations that lead to feelings and self-knowledge?"

Information about the everyday lives of West Berliners had just been reported to East Berliners. Jubilation would be delayed until the shock, resentment, fury, and sadness subsided. It would be some time before their response was hopeful and forward-looking.

I was struck by the resemblance of this reaction to the one I experienced in corporations undergoing transformation. It turned out that transformation wasn't a flash in the pan. There were phases and stages that emotional expression traveled before coming to the happier, new vision first proposed. These stages were understandable and even "mappable."

WORKING WITHIN THE CORPORATE BODY

Around this time, a new field of discipline called "organizational development" (OD) was emerging. It was devoted to the study of business environments, the change process, and the leadership required to facilitate change. Authors Terry Deal and Allan Kennedy coined the term "corporate culture" in their 1982 book by the same name, and it marked the beginning of marketplace acknowledgement that the invisible Collective Force was a growing factor in business success.

The premise of OD was that because corporations were collectives powered by humans, and humans develop and grow, so do the corporations. Before the advent of this discipline, businesses still believed people were replaceable cogs in a wheel, and their individuality was fairly irrelevant to production and outcomes.

Over the next decade, new models and tools would emerge that assured workers' voices were heard and included in strategy development. As I got to know colleagues who were pioneering this discipline, trying to convince corporate leaders of its legitimacy, I joined in the effort.

Using its principles in my independent consulting with some success, I began teaching as adjunct faculty at the University of San Francisco in the master's program in organization development and human resources. While consulting and teaching, I also started a practice I called "Healing Insight," in which I used my intuitive abilities to sense the cause of clients' angst and articulate it.

At times my hands would move without my permission, and when they did, my client would often sigh in great relief as if I had released something burdensome with one sweeping gesture. At that time I was not in touch with the understanding or meaning behind my hand movements, but I allowed them in Healing Insight sessions, as they seemed to be helpful.

At one point I met with a woman who described herself as a "psychic and energy practitioner."

She said to me, "When you are working in businesses, and you are up in the front of the room, you pin your hands behind your back."

I laughed. "Yes, I do that! If I didn't, my hands would go all over the place."

"Well, stop that," she replied. "The movement of your hands is sweeping away old energy in the room and helping people become clearer as they release old beliefs and patterns."

You could have knocked me over with a feather! From that point on, I moved my hands with abandon as I facilitated organizational change. Oddly, I also got a reputation for taking my shoes off when I worked with a group. I told them it was because my feet hurt in the heels I was wearing. The truth was that in order to ground the often chaotic and volatile energy in the room, I needed to feel my own feet firmly planted on the ground.

As my journey of embodiment progressed, I assumed that my consulting, in part, would help people become aware of energy in the room, and encourage them to "stay" to uncover what might emerge from that silence. I was astonished to find that in my next consulting engagement I would offer my client business leader the opposite advice!

STOP MEDITATING AND GET BUSY

Brian was referred to me by another client for whom I had facilitated a strategic planning process. He was opening a small resort focused on business-meeting facilities. He was amply funded through a business partner who did not want a hands-on role. I supported him as a business consultant in both thinking through his vision as well as working with others to make his dream a reality. Brian was not schooled in business, but he was a highly intuitive person and a practiced meditator.

There were many practical, everyday decisions to be made, from the resort service offerings to the individual décor of the units. The leadership team made most of those decisions, while the final review was left to Brian. I helped him think through the options, opportunities, and the potential consequences of diverse choices, and was liaison with other leaders and their requirements and requests.

Sometimes Brian received conflicting information or opinions from his leadership team, and he had a hard time deciding what to do. So he would meditate.

While I respected this as a way to be clear and receive information that would be helpful, meditation turned out to be his exclusive way of decision making, sometimes grinding operations to a halt until he was finished. When it was time to make a key decision as the resort opening date drew closer, Brian decided to go on a ten-day silent retreat.

It was then I said, "Brian, your intuition led you to this vision, and it looks like you are going to realize it. That's great news. However, this has been a slower process than it needed to be because you don't know whom to trust and you aren't always intuitively clear to respond to every decision you have to make.

"In the long term, operational success requires informed confidence—you either trust the people you hire or you trust your own decisions. My suggestion is that you take some business courses and learn how to ask intelligent questions so that you can support your intuition and build greater trust in others' competence. You can't be successful when your fear leads the way."

Brian did not follow my recommendation and went instead to his retreat. So I amiably left my consulting role at that point.

The resort did open—a couple of years later, and under different ownership.

I learned that when relying on intuition or inner guidance alone, follow-through and sustainability are unlikely outcomes. On the other hand, if analysis has authority as the only guide, success is possible—while feelings of emptiness and meaninglessness prevail.

It is only when decisions are factually infused and intuitively informed that inspired production is possible.

CHANNELING THROUGH HEAVY METAL

While having to defend the traditional business model with Brian, in the next consulting engagement, I found myself on the extreme other side of the coin.

One of my former master's students asked me to consult with her Fortune 500 Company, which made heavy-metal equipment. Specifically, Melissa asked me to design and facilitate her department's retreat in preparation for reorganization. This was to be one of the most unique blends of using both intuitive gifts and business consulting that I had experienced.

Melissa told me that her group was progressive, and if my intuitive work seemed appropriate at any time, I could employ that "methodology." I gently informed Melissa that I would only go to the level of permission in the group. That is, if even one person was the least bit uncomfortable with the use of intuitive information or methodology, I would apply the usual organizational development principles. When she specifically polled the group, she said only Sally had some doubts. Then she said that Sally was willing to talk with me about it. Melissa said Sally wanted to meet me at the bar of the hotel when I checked in.

I could feel Sally's eyes rolling from the minute I walked toward her. As I had no attachment to influencing or convincing others to buy into my map of reality, I assumed it would result in facilitating the retreat through "business as usual" tools.

Staring mostly at the drink in her hand, Sally began cynically, "So you're the psychic. Tell me something I don't know about myself."

The few times I have been addressed this way have made me feel like a trained monkey without his organ grinder. I simply wanted to say, "If you are uncomfortable with the application of intuition, I am perfectly fine facilitating the retreat using the OD tools with which you are familiar."

Instead, what came out my mouth—much to my own surprise— was: "Your brother never meant to hurt you and he really wants your forgiveness." Sally's eyes widened, and she stifled sobs as she quickly left the bar. She looked back for a moment and blurted out, "Use whatever gifts you want. I'm fine with it!"

I had no idea what was happening between Sally and her brother; I didn't even know Sally had a brother! I continue to believe that when any of us surrender to the God of our heart, and asked to be used in service to others, Spirit sometimes speaks without asking our permission or without consulting us on whether we approve of the results. And so it was with Sally.

Reviewing my carefully completed design of the program using the creative tools of OD, I began the first day of our three-day retreat with a silent and familiar prayer: "May I channel Christ's blessings in the work we do together for the highest good of all those involved, including the organization and its future." Little did I know that this time the prayer would be answered in a more direct way than I had ever known.

During the retreat, I felt as though I were watching a foreign movie, with English subtitles. It was a running ticker tape of unspoken information streaming into my consciousness as subtext to the conversations at hand. This was very different from the hyper-vigilance I usually apply to observing the group's dynamic, feeling my way through a facilitating style that continually asks: "What wants to happen next?"

Typically I am in the same "I don't know" soup as participants. My job is to create an environment and design that encourages generative dialogue—the kind of conversation and learning that happens when we reflectively listen to each other. While that is what I assumed I would do, I discovered something more powerful in the moment.

As one of the participants received a phone call from a top leader who wanted several members of the assembled group to quickly address an urgent priority, I felt my body begin to relax as a spiritual Presence emerged around me. It reminded me of the Presence of Christ I'd felt in my childhood. The Presence loomed very close to my ears and eyes, and there was no doubt its purpose was to be used in extraordinary service to this group. Within seconds I Knew that this Presence contained absolutely no judgment, only intimate compassion, profound respect, and a clear understanding of each individual's uniqueness. I felt deeply humbled.

Having completed the top leader's task, as the group reassembled, I did my best to simply get out of the way so this Love could find its mark in the heart of each participant. It did not matter that the business agenda was supporting heavy-metal product production. The Presence was there in response to this courageous group that had invited in learning at a personal as well as professional level.

At one point, around the end of the second day, in the middle of Don's response to a query, I heard myself say to him, "Stop. You are not with yourself. Remember what happened when you were a boy of seven years old and you sat in front of the mirror. I will come back to you." Then I called on the next person.

The authority that came though me was not how I know "me." I wouldn't interrupt. I wouldn't refer to personal information in front of a group. I most certainly wouldn't tell someone something about himself in front of a group—or even privately, unless he specifically solicited it. I often facilitate with an awareness that I want to gently check in to see whether others notice what I am noticing. I would call it "a respectful approach."

This was clearly an authoritative "I Know" approach that pointed out not only personal information but also information that was not intended to be revealed through either the official agenda or with conscious permission from the person addressed. Yet, different from the traditional corporate, top-down "tell," this was coming from a place that Knew Truth for each person. Astonishingly, no one balked or showed surprise or outrage at this out-of-context comment at a business meeting. I flashed back to the time I had been late for class in high school and what I had learned about trusting Who ordered reality.

When I returned to Don, "I" asked with the same authority, "Do you remember now?" Don said, "Yes. It came back to me. I remember being seven years old and being really mad at something that happened. I found a bag. I sat in front of a mirror. And I told myself I was going to stuff all my feelings into this bag—and I would never tell anyone again what I was feeling." Then he said, "And I haven't. Until now."

He stopped for a moment. "It's time for me to take my feelings out of that bag." Then he wept for a long time. The other participants were moved with compassion, but did not comment or even move uncomfortably. Others had their own tale when it was their turn.

While it seems, reading these paragraphs, that I allowed this business meeting to turn into a therapy circus, the group thoroughly addressed and wrapped up all the business agenda items in preparation for reorganization—only now each person was also clearer about what deep, personal reorganization meant for him or her.

At the end of the retreat, which occurred on Good Friday of Christians' Holy Week, I was shocked when each and every person came to me separately and apologized for taking all the time for their personal needs at the expense of the others.

What occurred to me was the New Testament story in the Bible of the loaves and fishes. In that passage, there were a few loaves and fishes, and five thousand people to feed. Christ blessed the food, and despite the meager resources, every person received what they needed and ate to the full. In fact, leftover scraps were collected and filled twelve baskets.

My prayers for Christ's blessing to come through in this retreat were answered—by the invitation, willingness, and receptivity of the whole group.

CORPORATIONS COMING OF AGE

By the mid-nineties, the marketplace had shifted its Collective Force from a map whose organizing principle was production, with all other functions bowing to it, to one where the central questions became these: What is our unique identity? Through what values do we choose to work together? Where are we going? How can we be the best?

These questions directly reflected what individuals ask as they mature: Who am I? To what do I aspire? What is my purpose? With what values will I engage others? I was excited to be part of this corporate coming of age.

At this point, OD gained new cache as leaders saw statistics that showed over 90 percent of corporate attempts at enterprise-wide change were failing—largely due to the human factor.[1]

Studies I reviewed as I undertook a PhD in organizational transformation found that when workers' emotional responses to significant change went unattended, sabotage, rumor mills, and all manner of energy-sapping strategies followed—all of them negatively impacting bottom-line results. If companies could not find ways to systemically address this seemingly strange new phenomenon of the human element, they would continue to lose hundreds of millions of dollars.

OD came to be called "change management" and later spawned the currently robust coaching industry. OD adapted the grief model of Elizabeth Kubler-Ross, MD, who opened up the field of grief counseling and who identified the emotional stages of grief. Partners Dennis Jaffe, PhD, and Cynthia Scott, PhD, referred to Kubler-Ross when they created an "organizational change model" that offered

---

[1] (65) Grover, Varun, and Seung Ryul Jeong, William Kettinger and James Teng, "The Implementation of Business Process Reengineering" Summer 1995, *Journal of Management Information Systems,* pp109-144

leaders a way to productively respond to workers' emotions during times of significant change. As workers let go of a familiar company culture, they move through stages of loss, anger and chaos before they can begin to understand what the new culture requires and commit to supporting it.

In working with companies undergoing transformation, I found that it was becoming increasingly important to know these stages of emotional expression. After years of working in this area, I found that facilitators of deep change have to clearly understand their jobs, or they can inhibit or prolong the process.

ALL THE VOICES ON THE TABLE

My first experience in facilitating large-scale change came when I accepted a position at AT&T's West Coast office. This was three years after AT&T's initial divestiture, and this opportunity was entirely unrelated to the work I'd done as part of a big six consulting firm's engagement on the East Coast.

The timing was synchronistic because as an outside consultant, I had grown frustrated when clients would change ideas, agendas, and project status without giving me the reasons. I wanted to learn to turn a team around from the inside out, using the politics of the process as part of the transformational fuel. As an intuitive, I wanted to be in a position to design processes that brought marginalized, hidden voices to the planning and decision-making tables.

One day, an officer, Ted, called me to help turn around his 2500-person organization, starting with the sales and sales-support functions.

Many workers had been in their jobs for decades, doing laudable work—yet did not know the work accomplished by the person located two desks over from them. This was a time before the word "transformation" became the norm for describing significant change.

Since OD was a rather new discipline, and often dismissed as a means of playing fun games for "team building," I decided on an anomalous approach. I requested that Ted leave me alone for six weeks and let me work with his sales-support organization. If the results were not to his liking, he could fire me from working in his division and give me a poor performance review. If we hit the mark with his expectations, then we could expand the methodology to other parts of the organization. I would stay within budget and give him early warning if there were any significant challenges. He agreed, and I got to work.

After the announcement that I would be working with the group, I talked to the whole group about the objectives of the change. Specifically, I let them know that I believed the answers for the way to increase productivity, quality, and customer focus were within them, and not in outside experts. Then I trained a core group of fifteen to twenty people on interviewing skills and collecting data from colleagues. When the group returned from their interviews with data in hand, we combed through the volumes to find patterns, connections, and meaning.

For participants, a process like this is akin to going through old photo albums after someone close to us passes. The core group not only has the opportunity to hear their colleagues' voices together for the first time, but they also have the unhappy privilege of feeling all the emotions that occur in that process.

Before the group found new strategies for moving forward, they would face, through the data, every complaint they'd ever felt and voiced, or hadn't; they would see that "the way we have always done it won't work anymore"; they would despair at the prospect of their familiar world dying. And then, there is that fragile moment where grace and hope or hopelessness determines whether the new life will see the light of day.

We were meeting from six thirty to eight a.m., three days a week for six weeks, after which the group dispersed to start their regular job. In the third week, as the core group was determining the "findings" based on all the data, one of the participants said loudly, "My husband works at a bank. They are going through the same kind of thing as we are. But they did it differently. It didn't take all this time and hassle, and it wasn't this hard."

Clearly the gauntlet had been thrown. It was six thirty-five a.m., and I am not a morning person. When I worked at Tarrytown, I told the chairman that if he was to receive the biggest bang for his buck, he should start all meetings at nine a.m. when my brain actually began to work.

"In early meetings," I warned him, "I walk very slowly and I talk very slowly."

His response was swift: "You talk more slowly? Pam, schedule all our meetings for six a.m."

So there I stood in front of this group as they awaited my response. Before I could speak, Dan piped up: "I know. One of my friends said the same thing about what they are doing at work. This design isn't working. We aren't getting anywhere with this."

Just before I let these comments hurt my feelings, I remembered that this is the phase of emotional expression in a change process known as "Kill the Consultant Time." It signals that fragile, critical point at which the group may opt out of the process and leave without satisfying results or, alternatively, take ownership for the process and outcomes. Here is the most important moment in facilitation.

"Sounds like you guys know other methods that are more helpful and productive than this one," I finally responded.

They began to nod, now with a bit of self-righteous satisfaction.

I said, "Geez, if I had poured as much time into a process as you have into this one, and it wasn't working, I'd feel pretty angry." I stopped. No one moved. "Does anyone here feel that way?"

Looking down at the table in front of them, a couple of workers nodded. Finally, Gus said rather quietly, "Actually, yeah, this is pretty maddening. I mean, I'm taking all these hours out of my personal time and I'm coming here three times a week and for what? Yeah, I'm angry."

I walked to the flip chart and wrote "Angry."

Then I said, "You're right. This is a lot of personal time...and I know some of your coworkers are taking on extra work for you to be here. Frankly, if this really isn't working, I'd be mad as hell."

People looked up and nodded, more willing to show their emotional cards. Trish said, "Well, look, I am mad. But I'm also worried. Our department is counting on us, and we're failing them. What are we supposed to say about all the resources we're taking to do this?"

I wrote "Mad" and "Worried."

George followed, "Hey, there is just too much data, and there's no way we are going to get to where we thought we would. We don't have enough time. This is completely hopeless."

I wrote "Afraid" and "Hopeless."

At this point, I stopped talking. If I had said anything at this juncture, I would have been saving, rescuing, or letting my ego take over to soothe the team and the situation. These workers were currently self-identifying as victims of a plot to make them the fall guys for their upcoming organizational change disaster.

It was a very long, uncomfortable silence. It's important to understand the power of silence in the process—especially in the United States. Once I went to an international conference, and a woman from an Asian country said, "You people in America think that when silence occurs, the conversation is over. In my country when silence occurs, the relationship has finally begun."

What I've learned is that groups can stand silence for about a minute or maybe two, and then someone will feel compelled to break it. The person who speaks first is often a very empathic person who can feel all the tension and fear in the room. He or she is compelled to "name that feeling" or address it with a resolution in order to relieve his or her own inner emotional overwhelm. This can be perceived as a helpful and courageous expression, or it can cause others to distance themselves from the speaker, and remain in denial of their own feelings.

At this point, the process can break apart or it can break through. There are no guarantees.

In this case, it was Jeff who, rather than only name the emotional tenor, decided to add his resolution: "Look, I know this is frustrating and seems impossible. I've been thinking we just can't get this done in time. But our coworkers are counting on us. We can't let them down. We have been working on this over three weeks! If we can't figure this out, then who can?"

I said nothing, allowing the group to decide how they felt in relation to this statement.

Jessie added, "We are on the hook for this. If this has been a complete waste of time, then we go back to the people who have been covering our work for us an hour a day on top of their own work and explain it to them. They keep wondering what we're doing in here. Somehow we've got to finish this and show something for their effort and ours."

Slowly those who had been staring at the table in front of them nodded hesitantly, without looking up. I waited without encouraging them.

This is the moment where ownership shifts. If they all agree, then this project becomes theirs and they take pride in it. If they don't have the courage to go to the next level of responsibility as a group and forge the path through unchartered territory, then it falls apart. The times when things fall apart are often marked by a group pointing to a consultant's poor design and facilitation, and excusing themselves of responsibility for process or outcome.

While it may well be that design and facilitation are primary contributors to poor outcomes, I have also known teams who consciously decided to take over a broken process and find a way to forge ahead to achieve their outcomes despite poor facilitation and design.

After more silence, Tom moved his chair closer to the table and looked around the room. He was a man of few words, but others listened whenever he spoke.

"OK," he said, "what do you say we get back to work?" And everyone else moved their chairs closer to the table—and this time, their nods were ones of conviction.

For me, this is the highest and best moment of my participation with the group. It is even more important than the actual outcome, because from that moment forward, the group is now a true team whose work represents something bigger than any of their individual sacrifices.

Their work is now in service of a more important goal. They will make their coworkers proud and create something that will be a win/win for them and the organization. Their decision to secure ownership of the process also indicates that they completed the change process's phases of denial, resistance, and chaos, and that they are at the beginning of "commitment" to the new way.

Having named and honored their emotional resistance, the team made fast progress after that point. All their vulnerability and fears had been named and faced as a group. There was nothing to stop them from doing their best work together. They no longer had to have thoughts about what another member thought of them. They had stated that they were "all in this together."

The team presented their results to the officer, using language that indicated their clear understanding of what was required for customer satisfaction and successful organizational outcomes.

Their recommendations included, among other things, changes to the nature of their own and their coworkers' jobs, the way the work flowed from beginning to end, and a plan and time frame for implementing their recommendations. Ted was speechless. He looked from them to me and back several times. "How did you get them to do this? How did you get them to know all this so fast?"

I said, "Ask them. They are the ones who collected the data, reviewed it, decided what it meant, and determined these conclusions. They did it. They just needed all the information on the table."

REFLECTION

The new experiences I had in business demonstrated to me the potential for new alignment when body and spirit are equally honored. I learned it was important to be balanced between the tools and rules of a trade and inward spiritual focus.

Using the body's sensations as a way to know when the energy of an entire group or organization is ready to move, and then using methods of change management to facilitate that change, was thrilling. I became fascinated with how an entire Collective Force could be transformed.

When I thought about my childhood experience of Oneness and this new experience of individuality—seemingly apart from the whole—I wanted to further sort out and understand the dynamics and power between the individual and the whole in transforming Collective Forces.

CHAPTER EIGHT

Nailing Down Beliefs

Over my five years of working as an internal consultant with AT&T, the leaders and professionals with whom I worked often sought me out to provide insight for personal challenges. Eventually, in my off hours, I began to do formal Readings that imitated some of the characteristics I had observed in working with Judy at Psychic Horizons, adding my own brand of values and nuances. During my last year with AT&T, I relocated from the Bay Area back to Chicago. Then within another year, AT&T "trivested" and offered me a severance package, which I joyfully accepted.

I began consulting independently again, offering intuitive Readings as a separate business. I continued to be intrigued by the dynamics of change and how the body/mind/spirit connection worked in relation to the power of thoughts, fear-based beliefs, and convictions.

In search of answers, I attended a seminar that featured a pioneer of holistic health who demonstrated what is possible when the mind is consciously directed. In 1958, Jack Schwartz founded Alethia Foundation, dedicated to "self-health research and education to bring forth the integration of body, brain, mind, and spirit." In the sixties,

Schwartz participated in experiments with Dr. Elmer Green at the Menninger Foundation. In one of these experiments, Jack put a long sailmaker's needle through his biceps. No blood appeared. Schwartz said he thought of his arm as "an arm," not "Jack's arm." He considered himself "a bundle of consciousness," stating that "bundles of consciousness do not bleed."

Dr. Green asked Jack if he could make his arm bleed. When describing what happened in retrospect, Jack said that after thinking about Dr. Green's request, he felt fear, and his attention moved from his higher self to his ego or self-image. His wound opened up like a faucet. Upon seeing the blood pour down, Jack understood what had occurred.

He said, "I moved back into silence, identified with my higher self, and the bleeding stopped instantly." Jack demonstrated that he could regulate other internal states as well, such as blood pressure and heart rate.

I met Jack Schwartz at a conference before he passed away in 2000. In addition to listening to him teach about alignment with the Divine in thought and action, I heard him say that he was selling his own line of vitamins. He laughed as he said, "Now, I don't take these vitamins because I do not believe in them. Other people, however, put their trust in things outside themselves, so why not sell them what they believe in? And then they will feel better!"

The work and writing of cellular biologist Bruce Lipton, Ph.D, can be used to support Schwartz's assumptions about how he was able to control his internal states. In his powerful books called *The Biology of Belief* and *The Tapping Solution*, Dr. Lipton states that the body's internal environment influences the way in which cells develop into different tissues. And what are the strongest determiners of environment? Dr. Lipton says it is not DNA, but our beliefs!

His work goes further and demonstrates that even our existing genes and DNA can be manipulated by our beliefs. What if the current and pervasive scientific studies that are part of the Collective Force that has concluded our condition is purely related to our DNA, and that the only solution is to medicate, moved closer toward Dr. Lipton's conclusions? Schwartz's and Lipton's conclusions seemed to indicate that any freewill belief we practice to the point of conviction can reorganize the physical state of our bodies.

As I pondered the relationship between body and belief, I realized Hakomi's philosophy complemented this conclusion. Hakomi methods help us get in touch with the often uncomfortable sensations and feelings that our body is holding. Then it helps us unravel the underlying beliefs that we have unconsciously adopted that are limiting our emotional and/or physical health. Schwartz speaks to the other side—how positive beliefs further our health.

Of all the studying I had done since my Dark Night began, I concluded that the beliefs we hold dear are the most potent ingredient shaping the quality of our lives. And so emerged another question. How do beliefs play into our relationships with each other?

Remembering the incidence at Psychic Horizons when one stranger strongly and suddenly influenced my feelings, I questioned what beliefs he possessed about me and about the situation. I also recalled the complete conviction I had when I was young that my father's situation with his dental assistant could be changed within twenty-four hours.

Did my strong belief more potently influence the outcome than if I had said a kind prayer laced with hope?

Furthermore, I wondered, "What happens when many people's beliefs are in contrast to one person's belief?"

RAISE YOUR ARM IF YOU AGREE

To address these questions, I decided to do an experiment to measure the impact of one person's belief on a group, and a group belief's impact on an individual. At the time, I was teaching a class at the University of Chicago Graham School entitled "Leadership from the Inside Out," and was emphasizing the importance of self-awareness for business leaders. I informed participants that we would be discovering more about being self-aware leaders through an exercise, and wondered whether Schwartz's and Lipton's conclusions would play out in this environment.

I asked a volunteer, Jim, to leave the room while I instructed the rest of the room to think positive or negative thoughts about him on my signal. I would find out about Jim's unconscious response by using kinesiology, a term that means "the study of movement in the human body." Often called "muscle testing," it is a practice used by many health practitioners to test the body's physical alignment or its level of acceptance for particular supplements, vitamins, or medication.

Jim said he had not previously heard of muscle testing or kinesiology. I asked him to extend his left arm while I stood behind him, facing the rest of the class. Then I requested that he hold his left arm strong without straining, as I pushed down on it, just below his elbow. That gave us a baseline indication without bias about how strong his muscle was.

Another volunteer, Sue, then came up and took my place to assure that I was not biasing the results, and she did the same test on the participant, with the same result of strength. Upon request, Jim closed his eyes, and I told him we were just going to repeat the same test. At that point, I held up my right hand to signal the class to think negative thoughts about Jim. The test was clear. Jim's arm dropped like a rock, and he himself said, "Wow, I don't know what happened there."

I replied, "Well, let's try it again and see if we get a different result."

As Jim closed his eyes again, I signaled the class to think positive thoughts. Jim's arm, by his own account, was even stronger than the first time or baseline.

That test may seem obvious to many. Our daily wellbeing is influenced by how those around us feel about us. Kinesiology tells us that this is not just the reaction of a particular muscle to a situation, but it is indicative of a weakened immune-system response. The negative thoughts of others are actually affecting our health.

While that is an interesting point to consider, an even more important lesson comes in what happened next in class.

I gave Jim a card that said, "I am really embarrassed to be up here. I feel like a fool. This is just awful." I asked him to concentrate on the feelings that were written on the card, without telling the other participants the message.

As Jim closed his eyes, I signaled to the class to think positive thoughts about Jim. Clearly, twenty-five people constituted more energy charge than Jim alone did. So the expectation was that Jim's arm would be strong, as he felt the invisible support of the whole room. However, that did not happen. Jim's arm dropped like a rock again.

I said, "Well, before we talk about this, let's try one more thing."

I gave Jim another card with these words written on it: "I feel successful and strong. I am the best thing since sliced bread. I am the happiest and most confident I can be right now."

Asking Jim to feel those words as though they were real to him, I signaled the other participants to think negative thoughts about him. They did. Again, a room full of negative thoughts ought to trump one single positive thought. But Jim's arm was as strong as a rock.

The class discussed what might be behind the results. They concluded that a thought field, whether coming from this group or a society of people, can only impact an individual if he remains unaware of his power. When he chooses to be conscious about what he is thinking, or to become self-aware, then his thoughts prevail. Then we discussed the consequences of these conclusions on leaders and their businesses.

"Self-aware leaders," Jim commented, "can prevent workers' negativity from influencing their thinking."

"Yes," I replied. "And here is the next question: What is necessary for a leader to not only maintain his personal power but also to use it to change a Collective Force in his company?"

While Jim, as well as the heroes of my old consulting firm, maintained their power in opposition to the prevailing negative Collective Force, they did not become the force for changing it.

Can the consciously chosen belief of an ordinary person change a Collective Force? I thought about what happened for the workers at

AT&T when they moved from fear to conviction to collectively changing the business culture. Was Jeff, the first worker to decide to speak out and commit to a new direction, the linchpin to the change? Did his belief create a domino effect that became the impetus for changing the whole business culture? If so, how did he acquire that power?

In searching for answers to these questions, I went to historical figures whose lives informed my inquiry.

THE ACT OF INFLUENCING A COLLECTIVE

It is well-known that as a lawyer working in South Africa, Gandhi was mistreated because of his ethnicity. It was his response to this treatment that went against all prevailing paradigms of justice. He refused again and again to strike back or even press charges against those who beat him and abused him to unconsciousness.

He would stage protests with fellow Indians regarding the unfairness of such acts by the South African government that declared only Indians had to register their identity and fingerprints or be jailed or deported. As he made his individual acts of protest and still the injustices continued, the power of his beliefs grew stronger. He quit being a lawyer so that he could devote his time to fighting injustice outside of court.

As his conviction gained power, action followed. As I was reading about Gandhi's activities, it occurred to me that when action follows strong belief, it not only tells the unconscious mind that "this is real," but it also demonstrates to others that there is something that "matters" about it.

Subatomic physics tells us that there is no such thing as physical matter. Everything and everyone is composed and comprised of energy. Energy becomes matter as intention and attention are persistently focused. Eventually we are engaged in "matters of importance" to us. It follows then that persistent action based on sustaining beliefs builds a personal field of energy, which creates what we commonly call "presence."

Gandhi's repeated actions based on strong convictions were in service to the same objective: to change the prevailing map of reality. He fasted, spent time to jail, took on the clothes of the most humble of his countrymen, and continued to voice his truth without violence or revenge. It seems that when others witnessed these consistent actions, it touched something inside of them that they had been silently desiring to become "real."

As more of his countrymen joined him, the energy, translated into action, began to move. Sometimes this movement was called or translated as "civil disobedience."

I pondered those words. What I found interesting was that the energy of the word "disobedience" contains "against" energy. In Gandhi's case, it sent a clear message about what was "factual" at the time—that there was a "bigger other" who made the rules, and that Gandhi wanted to organize against it.

If that were the only way the movement had been known, I believe it would have been less successful. "Against energy" is an investment of mental, emotional, and physical energy so that there is not enough time or resources left to build or sustain a new paradigm.

Opposing "the way things are around here" is often the way people start to move away from paradigms they can no longer abide, whether it is their family of origin or their faith tradition. "Against energy" represents the first sign or awareness that the status quo is no longer acceptable. It directs our emotions to feel anger and outrage toward the limitations of the prevailing map of reality and its boundaries, because anger mobilizes us. Now we can stand apart from what was once part of our skin.

Anger separates us from our environment and makes it visible from its traditionally invisible and subtle impact on us. Now we can ask questions because, for the first time, we know we have a choice. This can be a point of growth and individuation, a time to choose personal authority over those who have held position-power over us. However, we must eventually give up "against energy" because the investment distracts us from realizing positive purpose.

Gandhi's movement later became known as "nonviolent protest." While the word "protest" also describes a motive in relationship to someone or something else, it is softer and seems to assume that the "other" has less authority over us than when the word "obedience" is used.

As the movement grows, the Collective Force is beginning to make itself known, learning that it can now launch its own opinion rather than simply "not comply" with a larger rule. Further growth is required to build a sustainable paradigm as the energy of "protest" still bows to another master.

What Gandhi first called his personal intent, and the one that was the most powerful in the end, was "Satyagraha," or to "seek truth." This action does not consider the opinions of, power of, or relationships with others but stands instead upon its own strength, its own voice. Gandhi believed that if he sought the truth as he knew it, justice as he understood it would prevail and his mission would be realized. However, he did not limit himself to his private idea of truth and justice.

Gandhi was a spiritual man who was devoted to the Hindu deity Rama, referred to in Hinduism as Maryada Purushottama, which is literally translated "the Perfect Man," "the Lord of Self-Control," or "the Lord of Virtue." Since he was young, Gandhi had dedicated his work to Rama. He persevered in the face of horrendous odds because he believed his personal intent and actions were aligned with and supported by a higher truth.

How we hold our relationship with the Divine, or the higher good— whether we align with it or resist it—can be the most powerful element in creating a new Collective Force. In business transformation, it is well-known that without a vision and mission that is larger than any one faction in the company, change is not possible. The organizing principle of change must have an emotional component that appeals to our sense of the highest good or collective greatness.

I began to wonder what would have happened if Gandhi's intent had been to change the rules only to benefit his family. If that had been the case, he would have relied on his own energy, intelligence, and political savvy to influence power brokers. While that could have worked for him as easily as it does for anyone with those talents, I remembered what I learned from mystic experience—that when actions are disconnected from Source, emptiness and meaninglessness follow. Absent a vision and higher good, and with dependency upon ourselves alone to accomplish the goal, depletion and exhaustion are likely.

Awareness of our connection to what is larger than us inspires and sustains us, and can allow energy to come through us rather than from us. When we identify with that which is boundless and act in alignment with the guidance that springs from an authentic relationship with that limitlessness, we become an attractor field of positive influence for others.

Reading about Gandhi and his movement's progress from "disobedience" to "protest" to "seeking truth," I realized he was demonstrating phases of transformation—from resistance and chaos to searching for what belonged to the emerging vision to finding a new voice and presence that led the way to attaining the vision and mission.

Now I had a better understanding of how one person exercises beliefs and actions, grows his convictions into a shared movement, and becomes a presence that leads to a Collective Force for and with others. Moving forward, I wanted to know what then defines and holds together the new vision? Obviously, Rama represented the quality of self-control as one of the values Gandhi embraced. Is it these kinds of values that, when practiced, hold a new map of reality together?

This question stayed with me as I took a road trip that included a visit to my quirky, mega-successful cousin.

VALUES THAT DEFINE OUR POINT OF VIEW

Caitlin drove me from the train station to her home on the East Coast—the one that takes her away from her bustling Manhattan weekday life. Her circle driveway seemed longer than my high-school jogging track. Just as we got near the front door, I spied an object on the lawn that looked old and beaten-up. It was so entirely out of place that I thought my eyes deceived me.

"What's that?" I asked.

She replied, "Oh, that's a Clairol makeup mirror. Don't touch it. I garbage picked it, and I haven't figured out what I'm going to do with it yet. Isn't it GREAT?!"

My cousin goes to garage sales, flea markets, and yes, she still "garbage picks" with the best of them because she finds one-of-a-kind treasures that stir her design imagination.

It occurred to me that we individually assign value to certain things that would cause others to turn up their noses, and certain objects we find intolerable, others embrace. My thoughts on this subject were further inspired by an offbeat seminar I attended a month later.

Jack, our instructor, started by asking us to walk over to a nearby forest preserve and collect garbage—pieces we felt drawn to or that called to us. This process was not written in the course description! We dutifully combed the forest floor, and when we returned, he said, "Now tape your favorite garbage to one of these large canvases, and then spray-paint it in whatever colors you like." Spray-paint our favorite garbage?!

He continued: "Then un-tape the garbage, dispose of it, and collect more. Repeat this sequence until you feel complete." The thought of feeling complete by painting refuse made me laugh out loud. I thought

I was prepared for the messy outcome. However, when we were finished, lo and behold, this beautiful world showed up on the canvas, in overlapping, multicolored, celestial images. This incredible result came from "garbage picking"! Then Jack dragged in a large carton containing a multitude of frames.

"Now for the most important part," he said. "Pick any size or shape frame you want and then place it anywhere you like on the canvas—in the middle, upside down, or on the edges. The way you frame your creation is completely up to you."

When everyone was finished, we talked about what was inside our frame.

"Why did you include this circle but not that one?" Jack asked one participant.

"Oh, because then this part would be unbalanced and these circles really wouldn't fit together as well," replied Mark, as though this would be obvious to the most casual observer.

"Well, what if you moved it just slightly to the left and included this blue square?" Jack suggested.

"No, oh, no!" exclaimed Mark passionately. "That would throw everything off. Besides, I hate that blue square."

It was both funny and awesome to watch the ardent stories that arose from the echoes of garbage, and to hear the quick and sincere loyalty one aspect of an image secured, while another was self-righteously dismissed.

This is a form of art called "bricolage," a French word that means to "fiddle" or "tinker." In English, according to Webster, it implies "[to] make creative and resourceful use of whatever materials are at hand (regardless of their original purpose)."

Bricolage, as you may have guessed, is a metaphor for real life. Jack explained that we develop frames around our lives that are as instinctive as Mark's, unconsciously determining meaning driven by preferences whose sources are invisible.

"Your background, experiences, and education can increase or decrease the size of your frame, or influence where it gets placed in the scheme of your art," Jack remarked.

It occurred to me that it is our unique orientation that determines whether we seek out new understanding or relish the four sides of the frame that protects the bricolage of our beliefs and values.

"What you choose to put inside your frame is up to you," Jack continued. "Sometimes you get fixated on a particular situation, feeling, or life event, and no matter what else happens to other things in your frame, like Mark said, 'that one stays.' What you value lies inside the frame."

As I thought about the staying power of the values we choose, and their role in shaping the meaning of our lives, I began to wonder about what happens when many individual's values converge in a collective.

What are the impacts of a Collective Force when, for example, a company consciously chooses its values?

My next consulting engagement gave me the opportunity to design a process for assuring individual workers desires were an integral part of developing company values. And then I learned some completely unexpected answers to the question of how a values-driven Collective Force impacts the company!

PARTNERING WITH THE COLLECTIVE FORCE

The two-hundred-person Ohio manufacturing company with which I was consulting, participated in a process to identify their values. The values would be specifically chosen to support the new direction the company had recently formulated, and define how workers would choose to treat each other going forward.

For example, "open and honest communication" might replace the formerly closemouthed organization of the past where only the executive team discussed strategic information. Open communication would allow workers to inform upper management about customers' preferences and hear about strategic decisions under consideration.

In a full-day meeting, where the entire organization participated, I designed the room so that there was a maximum mix of departments and levels. For example, the chairman was seated next to a janitor at one of twenty tables. Through some carefully planned exercises, employees worked in pairs, engaged in table discussions, and then reported out to the whole group about what behaviors they believed were important at work. Then we talked about what values operated beneath these desired behaviors and worked until the entire organization chose and agreed to a list of thirteen values.

From there, volunteers who wanted to work to refine the list put their names into a box. We randomly picked seven people's names— one from each department—to form a "values team." The team's purpose was to solicit their colleague's input on the specific departmental meaning and impact that each value would have if it was chosen, and to then refine the values descriptions.

For example, when the production department discussed fairness as a value, they were referring to shift schedules, while marketing thought of fairness in terms of opportunities to work on high profile projects.

One of the volunteers, from the assembly and shipping department, was a Vietnamese man whose name, interestingly, is Sophia (So Pee a). When his name was announced, I remember thinking, "Hmmm. His name means 'wisdom'. I wonder what I'm going to learn from him." Little did I know what was about to happen!

"Sey," as they called him, was quiet and shy. With continual, gentle prompting over the course of the six weeks we spent together (a couple of hours per week), Sey grew more and more willing to participate. Like the other volunteers, Sey asked his peers what the production department would look like and/or what would change if the draft values were implemented.

Sey came back with a list of grievances from his peers—from a list of the tools they needed to do their jobs to a first-aid kit. A first-aid kit?

"What's up with that?" one team member immediately asked.

Sey replied, "Well, when we change the drill heads, the parts are old, and sometimes we cuts our hands and they bleed, and we don't want the blood to get everywhere."

I asked more specific questions while alarms continued to ring in my head.

While the team was upset about Sey's situation, they did not want "having proper tools and resources to do your job" and "safety" to become values for the whole organization. They wanted to fix the situation and asked me what to do. I asked Sey if I could get back to him in the afternoon, and he agreed. I talked with Ken, the department manager, about the situation, which he agreed to look into immediately.

I also suggested that since the intent of the new culture was to offer each other feedback, Sey could be part of the next executive managers' meeting and present his report. I would prepare the managers so they could be receptive. Ken thought it was a good way for the executives to walk their talk about the values of listening to honest upward feedback and addressing department needs more effectively.

I then talked with Sey about the idea. He felt intimidated and was quite reluctant, thinking they might shoot the messenger if he told them what the line workers were really thinking. It took a lot of courage for Sey to accept and prepare for such a public role, but at last he agreed.

At the managers' meeting, Sey was obviously nervous, shaking a little as he bravely and very quietly and slowly read what was on his list. While it was a bit longer and more involved than everyone anticipated, the managers were gracious and thanked him and his department for their honesty and for the information. They promised to follow up and congratulated him on his presentation.

There are few moments in years of work where even a small outcome brings the pride and gratitude this scene evoked in me. My jubilation at everyone stepping up to their ideals, however, was short-lived.

THE BIG SURPRISE

The week following this event, Dan, the general manager, made a surprise announcement—a completely unexpected production department layoff. He reported to the executive management team about who would likely be impacted—and Sey was on the list! As Dan informed the rest of the executive management team about his decision, I was at the table.

While in my professional role, I typically ask questions, help integrate information, or educate, in this moment I was direct: "YOU CAN'T LAY OFF SOPHIA!" I said vociferously. "He just demonstrated the value of honest upward feedback, and it was the first time in the history of this company that a line worker was heard like this. If you lay him off it will send a message to the organization that if you tell management the truth, you'll get fired!"

Joe said, "Sophia is the newest member of that department. Apparently we even gave him a day or two off to get married. Anyway, he's not our best performer, according to my leader in his area. He's out."

"If you do this, you could jeopardize the trust in leadership for a long time to come," I insisted. "No matter what you say about his position, people will remember that he bravely stood before you and told you the bad news, and then you fired him. And this is personal, too, because I encouraged him to do it. It looks like I set him up and you shot him—which was his worst fear! How can I continue to facilitate values implementation planned for the rest of the year? What will I say to them about the integrity of this?"

Dan said, "My team leader [Bob] identified Sophia as one of the last in, so he's one of the first out. Besides, he's not the best worker we have on the line. I can't tell Bob that because Sophia's name was picked out of a hat to be part of a team that he can't lay him off! That would mean that being on the values team protected him from what would otherwise be the case. It would send a bad message to his whole department and undermine Bob's authority and power."

We were now leaning over the table toward each other, eyeball to eyeball, both slightly red in the face. Dan and I were holding the power of two values whose impacts were both significant. They were equally important to the organization and how workers felt about their future in it: receiving honest upward feedback without reprisal, and being fair in how downsizings are implemented. How up meets down and down meets up. Representing the conscience of the organization, I insisted that each of the values had to be seriously considered.

The other managers were silent. No one wanted to touch this conversation.

I thought about how Sey had been picked for the team. A piece of paper with his name on it was chosen at random. On an everyday basis, his work relative to his peers was documented. Performance most certainly had to be given highest consideration, and the rules of last-in, first-out could not apply to everyone but Sey.

With both frustration and anger, I said, "You win on the values question." I sat back in my seat. "But I want to see the human resources documentation on Sophia's time, treatment, and training to assure that we have not left one stone unturned on another alternative." This was overreaching the bounds of my role, but Dan nodded. I was devastated. Dan was right, and yet this was the worst possible outcome for a newly "participative" organization.

Sey would not be the only person to consider. People had been accepting mediocrity at this company for so long that those who were rewarded in spite of bad performance were certainly not expecting any consequences at this point. The only helpful news was that the invisible territory of how and why decisions were made at the top became transparent and conscious. The leaders might feel terrible about the outcome, but they could honestly discuss with workers the criteria for decision making and the values that were considered.

Given the circumstances, I requested that the leadership provide an outplacement workshop for the production workers—a rarity in any company. They graciously agreed.

I reflected on his nickname and his first name: "Sey wisdom." What wisdom needed to be said now?

My business partner, Deb, got to work designing the workshop in which production workers would learn to write their resumes, practice interviewing, and learn how to network to find new positions. I decided to speak with Sey directly to explain the situation and see what I could do to support him.

Before I had the chance to meet with him, Deb called me and told me an incredible story.

"Sophia showed up at the first workshop. I let him know immediately that you were looking forward to talking with him and that I was so sorry for the layoff. Therese, he had a big smile on his face!"

"Had he been drinking?" I asked, as that was the only thing I could think that could possibly make him forget the pain of this situation.

Deb laughed. "No, he was happy. He said, 'I love this company.'"

"He was drinking," I declared bleakly, imagining my part in his lack of sobriety.

"No," she said, still laughing. "Listen to this! He told me that when he got married several months ago, his new wife wanted to move to Indiana where some of her family lives, but he had only recently secured work with this company. Then he got on the values team, and he said it taught him to speak up, and he learned how to represent his fellow workers. Now, he's going to get training to write his resume, interview, and get a job—in Indiana. He said, 'This is the best company I ever worked for!' He said he told everyone on the production line about this, and they were happy for him!"

"What are the chances of that?" I asked my partner.

At the next executive manager's meeting, I reported on Sey's story.

"How did we dodge that bullet?" asked Ken, shaking his head.

"Bottom line," I said, "when you really pay attention to values, it's not about getting it right. It's about knowing what your values are and which ones you are using to make the most important decisions. Keep the questions alive, and then, it seems, you get a little help from the spirit of the organization itself!"

The managers were relieved, grateful, and delighted. Values were firmly supporting their new direction within a new map of reality.

REFLECTION

Gandhi demonstrated that one individual can strengthen his influence by consistent and aligned action based on closely held values. Over time, persistence practice increased his power to the point where the prevailing Collective Force of a whole country was thrown into question. I was thrilled to learn about the potential power of one person!

In addition, Sey/Wisdom taught me that the intention to honor all the voices of a company and to work in integrity, holds its own Collective Force, which can then penetrate the reality in which normal business is conducted.

While I continued to enjoy business as a fascinating reality waiting to learn from its own members, intuitive Readings increased in volume.

PartII:
The Invisible Map of Reality

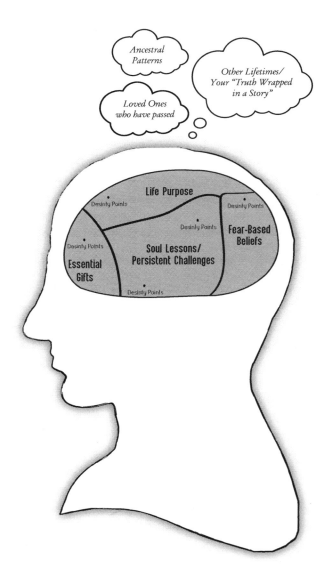

In Part II, I describe what I have learned from intuitively Reading clients. The content of their stories are slightly altered to mask their identity, except where express permission has been granted.

These particular stories illuminate the inner, hidden territories of our personal maps, as well as the connections among them. Collective Forces or outer influences that hold sway over our maps will be further explored.

Specifically, of the many outer influences, the focus is on three powerful areas: other lives/archetypes, ancestral patterns and loved ones who have passed. Because death is an inevitable experience in life and impacts us in ways our conscious mind cannot begin to grasp, I devote more pages to the world on the Other Side than to other outside influences.

Within our maps, the focus is on the exploration of five territories that include life purpose, essential gifts, soul lessons/persistent challenges, fear-based beliefs, and destiny points.

Before this exploration begins, chapter nine introduces the methodology and values used in Readings. I convey a client story that helped me understand the critical importance of inner listening to determine how to interpret the symbols that I perceive in clients' energy fields.

Reading Energy for the Living

It starts with the sound of someone's name. My most prominent gift is clairaudience ("clear hearing"). Each person's name is like music to my ears. When the client says her full name, it is as though she is opening the playlist of her experiences and showing me the songs that mean the most to her. Even though I don't know her Uncle Joe or Aunt Bessie, or why they mean so much to her, or even why she hates them, I am a sacred witness to her silent tales. I am willing to hear all that her invisible stories want to tell me.

Some people's energy reveal many pictures, stories and music all at once. When that happens, I move back and "hold the field," respecting that each of these elements has its place in the orchestra of my client's life.

As I continue to listen to the cacophony of sound and watch the moving pictures, I have unspoken questions: Which story is most urgently in need of being heard? What movement is most important in addressing my client's stated challenges?

As I wait patiently, one image often "lights up" in a specific area of the client's body, as if raising its hand to answer the questions posed. It is artwork that is welcoming my attention. As I begin to describe what I see, I sometimes come upon another image or story that I sense is important, but is shy or reluctant to come forward.

Per the Hakomi principles I learned in Boulder, I go only where I am invited. When a client's energy feels tight and reluctant, I say aloud, "I will not Read anything that you are not ready for me to See or that you do not want me to See. I'm only here to help with the challenges you want to show me." And, in line with those same Hakomi principles, the client's energy typically relaxes it fisted grip, unfolding more vivid pictures as it feels safer to divulge its secrets.

I am committed to describing the image exactly as I See it, however ridiculous, scary, or otherworldly it may sound, and then I "stay" with the same reverence I had in the chapel when I was in high school. With this discipline, something in the image shifts, and I describe what I See. After articulating it, I continue to hold that image's emerging story while I also scan for what else is happening in the field that wants to reveal itself.

When I Read clients' energy, I practice discernment, which is the skill of tuning into subtle distinctions to understand the truth and true nature of an abstraction, an archetype, or a set of symbols. Interpretation is inherent in this exercise.

One client's Reading dramatically reinforced what I learned from my bricholage seminar: the interpretive frame I embrace can make the difference between alienation and healing. It was a key learning in my practice.

IN POSSESSION OF AN OPTIMAL

INTERPRETATION

A straightforward woman, Germanic in bone structure, with long, blonde hair and a worldly air, came to see me. "I want to know about my son, Bill," she said flatly. "We have always been close, but not anymore. Four years ago, he married a woman I don't really care for, and he just stopped talking to me. I was really hurt, and I want to know what is going on. I have been to other spiritual counselors, but they couldn't help me."

I acknowledged her request, closed my eyes, and asked her to say her full name so that I could begin to Read her energy. Some initial images came through that resembled an airbrushed portrait—as though someone had combed through her image many, many times. This picture implied to me that Liz consistently worked to understand herself and chose to authentically grow through challenging situations.

"My impression," I said, "is that you are consciously aligned with your spirit and have been very attentive to your life lessons. It seems you have been seeking and finding ways to clear out old, unhelpful patterns and forge new paths."

Liz said nothing. While it is often the case that relationships are entangled in intricate ways, I sensed that this time there might be more going on with Liz's son than with Liz.

"May I look at your son's energy?" I asked. Liz agreed. Upon hearing Bill's full name, I tuned in and Saw an image that was wholly unexpected, and one that took me aback. It appeared as though three-quarters of Bill's body was inhabited by a mechanical, crab-like creature with many long, metal legs. It looked like something out of an old Star

Wars movie.

To encounter such an image was starkly new to me. In fact, it was so odd that I considered omitting this impression. I took a deep breath and reminded myself that I have a commitment to report the full truth of what I See. I said a silent prayer, asking for guidance in how to express this in a way that would be for Liz's highest good.

After a long silence, this is what came to me: "Your son does not want to take responsibility for a good deal of his life right now. He does not believe in himself or in his ability to 'be a man.' He has felt this deep sense of inadequacy for a long time and has organized his life around not acknowledging these feelings. He does not want to risk trying and failing. This is the way he is choosing to learn at the moment.

"Rather than feel his ongoing fear and shame," I continued, "Bill is 'renting out space' within himself to someone else's energy. This means that someone or something else is influencing him to continue to evade his responsibilities."

"In fact, I See an image inside his energy that looks like one of those creatures from Star Wars. You might even say it is 'alien energy.' However, it is also true that any energy that is not ours may be considered 'alien energy.' For example, if for my whole life, I insist on carrying around my sister's problems because it is easier than facing my own, or if I habitually throw myself into helping others so as not to face my own disappointments and loneliness, I'm carrying 'alien energy.' While some influences are stronger than others, the end result is the same—abdicating responsibility for some aspect of our lives.

"Furthermore," I continued, "the reason your son does not want to talk with you is that you have a very honest way about you. You deal with your fears and take responsibility for your life. Every time he is in your company, your example makes him more uncomfortable—and more aware that he has not done his human homework.

It may even be said that because your relationship with him is positive and close, he is not able to stand in your presence without facing himself in some way. And Bill clearly prefers not to face himself at this point."

Then I asked Liz's permission to take time out of her session to do some healing work with Bill. She quietly said, "Yes," with a touch of hope in her voice. After praying for his "renter" to leave, I asked that an angel cross his path to facilitate his healing. I prayed he would meet someone or something that would inspire him enough to face his fears and work through them, thereby reclaiming his power.

This is a different kind of prayer than one that simply asks for pain to subside. I could See that Bill was working on the quality of self-responsibility and that there were challenges with that. I believe, in this case, asking for Divine intervention so that the situation would simply go away would not be helpful to Bill's soul's desire to learn.

We are human beings not so that we swim in the happiness of having our desires fulfilled in every moment, though happiness is a wonderful part of life. We are here to do the human homework required to reclaim personal power and align with Love.

Having said that, I suggested that Liz pray for Bill, sending him positive energy and love for the next seventy-two hours.

I have found that three days after a Reading is a particularly powerful time. Many emotional releases and changes occur—from disorientation to grief to a lighter sense of self—as a person begins to align with their truth.

In Bill's case, he had not come to me for help. However, because Bill had the most precious gift of free will, if he was not ready to face himself or did not want to be influenced, the healing opportunity would simply go unnoticed or unrecognized. If he unconsciously accepted the healing, and that was accompanied by greater discomfort than he preferred, he might simply choose to call back his "renter." So there was no violation of his will in this exercise.

Tearing up with relief and sadness, Liz said, "My son quit his job and just stopped taking care of himself. He sits in his room and plays music all day. He lives off the small wages he earns from playing music gigs at night around the small town he lives in."

Liz was quiet for a moment, as if deciding whether she would continue. When she finally spoke, what she said next stunned me.

"A couple of months ago, I went to a Christian counselor, who was 'a Seer' like you. He did a Reading and told me my son was possessed by Satan and needed to be exorcised! I was so shocked and angry that I walked out of that room, slammed the door, and never went back."

INTERPRETATION OF GOOD AND EVIL

It was then that I learned a very important lesson about the nature of frames. I realized that the religious counselor had Seen something very similar to what I had, only he had pronounced it "evil." He interpreted this "creature" through a highly charged religious framework. The Seer was telling the truth from his interpretation about the invisible realms based on a Christian map of reality—and upon the discernment he utilized in that interpretation.

Through his map, he Saw this creature embedded in Bill's energy and referred to it as "possessed." I could completely understand and even agree that an alien energy had possession of much of Bill's energy. The difference was that because of the frame on the Seer's map, only a "man of God" could exorcize it. Certainly that excluded the possibility that Liz might be able to help her son, or that Bill could help himself.

My map of reality contains a different understanding of the word "evil." My interpretation stems from elements outside the boundary of Christian dogma. It stems from science as well as my experience with Spirit and intuitively Reading energy.

From science we know that our bodies are made up of the same cellular structure as the stars in our night sky. In fact, to the eyes of an intuitive who Sees, each of us shines and sparkles like a star—except when we are feeling afraid. Fleeting fear does not make a strong mark on an energy field. It is only the kind that is held dear and used as a basis for beliefs and defenses that becomes like a dark hole pulling in the natural light of our nature. Dark holes appear in the place in or around our bodies where we are holding onto fear. If we are overburdened with responsibilities, for example, the black hole may be near the shoulders, as we feel we are "shouldering responsibility" for others.

One interpretation of a black hole may be that is it "evil," which is, interestingly, the word "live" spelled backward. And fear does, in fact, cause us to live backward. To further the metaphor, these dark spots in our energy operate in much the same way as black holes in space.

Astronomers say that black holes, which are usually about three times the size of our sun, absorb anything on "the event horizon." This means that if our sun were to move near that horizon, the black hole would swallow our entire solar system in one gulp.

Black holes are very powerful. The reason scientists know where they are is because of the tremendous heat emanating from the explosions of objects and materials being absorbed. When afraid, humans also absorb, with anger and sometimes malice, the material that would otherwise enhance our light.

I told some of my young nieces about this, using the familiar example of some of the outrageously bawdy and drug-advocating celebrity singers, who seek applause and fame. Underneath their show, they likely fear they are unlovable.

In everyday situations, applause does add positive energy for well-deserved recognition. But with fear ruling the invisible map, applause becomes approval—an imitation of love—that serves the ego rather than fulfills the soul. Therefore, when the applause subsides, fear prompts further action to draw applause back to reassure the singer that his greatest fear of being unlovable is not true.

Addiction is born of trusting such substitutes for love, and the black hole continues to absorb the Light.

When it comes to the point where substitute-actions become habit, spirits that thrive in the dark simply reinforce that decision. They echo back the idea that trepidation is an important and reasonable response, and urge further action that aligns with fear as the best inner authority. The weight of these spirits can unconsciously be felt—indeed weight gain is not an unlikely development, representing this energetic truth—

and it can compel us toward depression.

Depression is a coping mechanism that allows us to avoid facing the weight within us that feels overwhelming. Medication that is ongoing, without an end in sight, then keeps us in that undifferentiated, unfeeling state, so that the possibility of discerning what is ours and what is not becomes more remote.

Eventually, and with permission through passivity or compliance, these spirits can take up residency. Liz's son was a man who abdicated most of his responsibilities and gave authority to his fear of inadequacy, allowing it to dictate how he lived his life. This was the most important territory on his map of reality. Therefore, "possession" is an appropriate term.

"Possession" is the result of a long-term and persistent choice to organize beliefs and actions around fear—whether consciously or unconsciously. This is more likely to occur when a person feels entirely detached from Source/Spirit, or any spiritual path. When there is a persistent disconnect between a person and his spirit, he may be described as a "lost soul." As you walk down the street, you might intuitively understand this when you look into someone's eyes and sense that "no one is home."

In his book *Power vs. Force, The Hidden Determinants of Human Behavior*, David Hawkins talks about the vibration of emotion. He explains that each feeling has a particular vibrational frequency—with fear/terror having the lowest frequency, and joy, the highest. When we act out of fear, we become ungrounded and abandon ourselves—because we don't want to "stay" and feel those uncomfortable vibrations.

In essence, we are expressing to the Universe/Creator through our free will that we are "not in possession of ourselves." Spirits that "attach" vibrate at the lower frequencies, reinforcing or amplifying our fear—and they grow more powerful in the dark of our denial.

While this description may sound scary, what is not well understood, I believe, is how an "evil force" or "spirit attachment" can be paradoxically helpful. There is the possibility that these entities and our choice to collude with them eventually cause us to feel so burdened and miserable that we pay attention and finally address the underlying fear. We can then reclaim the energy tied up in our defenses and begin to live life anew. And this, thankfully, is what finally happened to Bill.

FROM BLACK HOLE TO BECOMING WHOLE

Two years after my session with Liz, she returned to my office and asked, "Do you remember me?" I did not. She reminded me of the Reading and her son Bill. Then she said, "I must tell you what happened."

I felt a bit anxious. I was curious to know how her son was faring.

"Bill has always been an animal lover," Liz began. "He went outside one day to take out the trash and found a very sorry-looking dog near his apartment. The dog was mangy, underweight, and had clearly been abused—someone had sewn the dog's ears closed."

"Ow!" I said aloud, as I cringed at the thought.

Liz told me that Bill had taken the dog in, cared for him, and brought him back from the brink of death.

"As all this unfolded," she said, "he called me nearly every day to talk about the dog and discuss how to help him, since we are both animal lovers. We grew closer as a result of these conversations, and Bill slowly emerged from his darkness, little by little, day by day. He eventually got a job, picked up the pieces of his life, and now we are talking again."

I was heartened to hear her story, but before I could respond, she continued, "Therese, he found that dog three days after our session. That dog was the angel you prayed would come into his life."

"And," I found myself saying, "the dog's ears were sewn closed because it represented the part of your son that could not hear you, Spirit, or others who wanted to help. In healing the dog, Bill was ministering to and healing himself." As Bill privately cared for and loved the dog, he was free of others' expectations or judgments. And so he cared, he healed, he loved…and he received the same grace for himself.

When we pray or intend good things for another, Spirit designs what specifically resonates with that person's needs. Since we cannot know what form or frame this will take, it is essential to release attachment to how we think it should unfold. Thus we say at the end of all prayer, "Thy will be done." In this case, the God of Bill's heart knew that a dog at death's door would open up his heart and create a new possibility for reclaiming his power and his life.

Bill's map of reality didn't change because of the dog. The boundary of his map was broadened because of the decision he made to care for the dog—to go outside of his own world and his own needs. He was moving to the heart of what mattered to him through this relationship. As he expressed his love, his depression naturally began to diminish its hold, and he could grow in the direction of wholeness.

REFLECTION

Liz and Bill reminded me of what Jack, my bricolage instructor, had said: "The frame you decide upon makes all the difference." Following this Reading, I began to notice energetic consistencies in both inner maps and outer influences that swayed my clients to organize around a particular fear—and even demonstrate strong and often effective defenses to mask it. I began to suspect there was some kind of deliberate plan that was lurking just under our challenges, which if made visible, could inform us and then free us.

CHAPTER TEN

Influences that Shape the Boundary of the Invisible Map

This chapter speaks to the three influences that exist outside—yet overlap—a personal, invisible map of reality. Unless we are conscious of these influences and the wisdom they contain, they have the power to quietly influence our perceptions of reality and the kinds of choices we think we have. The three influences are: past lives (referred to as "your truth wrapped in a story"), ancestral patterns, and the Other Side.

YOUR TRUTH WRAPPED IN A STORY

When I'm Reading energy, after some time, the images I See unfold into stories that converge into themes. Visually, the stories are located behind a person. While I often call these images "past lives" because they come complete with specific roles within particular historical settings, more important to understand is that they are a client's "truth wrapped in a story"—an archetypal narrative, a piece of theater, a parable. Call it what you will, it is not relevant to me whether or not past lives exist.

As a Catholic, I was not raised to believe in reincarnation. However, when I was interviewed on the Dr. Oz radio show, the other gentleman who was interviewed on the same program was Jim Tucker, medical director of the child and family psychiatry clinic, and associate professor of psychiatry and neurobehavioral sciences at the University of Virginia. In his and Ian Stevenson's book, *Life Before Life: Children's Memories of Previous Lives,* he analyzed case studies of over 2500 children under the age of seven who recall historically accurate details of places they have never been and people they have never met. I was duly impressed as I listened to some of his findings.

Most interesting to me is that when I describe "other lives" in a Reading, clients are often extraordinarily impressed by their sense of familiarity or ease at relating to the role, responsibility, geographic place, giftedness, and/or qualities described.

While I could discern more particulars about the historical aspects of client stories, and in some instances those aspects have been very specific, in most cases it is not relevant to the Reading. Because the purpose of the Reading is to facilitate peace, the significance of the unfolding story is measured by how deeply my client resonates with how the character in the story makes meaning of his or her situation. Often there is a word, a feeling, or something in the story that is very specific for the client. When that word or feeling is articulated, I witness the client's energy relax the grip that holds fear as its prisoner.

For example, I told one client, Cindy, that in another life she owned a very special horse, which the neighborhood children loved. They begged her to let them brush and pet the horse. Cindy was an introvert, and it took some time before she agreed. Later, the children's parents convinced her to offer sleigh rides in the winter. Slowly, Cindy gave in to the pressure.

One day, the horse slid on some black ice and the sleigh tipped over, crushing one of the children's legs under its weight. The child was crippled for life. Cindy was horrified and felt entirely responsible. She immediately went back to her solitary life, and stopped letting the children near her horse in any capacity.

After I told that story and before I continued, Cindy interrupted with a loud inhale. "I can't believe this! I own a horse in this life. His name is Orie. I kept having this feeling that I wanted to do something for kids. So I decided to use Orie as a therapy horse for children with disabilities. Kids come out to my property and pet the horse. He's so gentle. We help the kids ride the horse, and they are so happy! How can this be?"

Cindy is still working out this other lifetime and finding ways to release her hidden guilt and shame. At some point in the Reading, we moved out Cindy's belief that she owes a debt to children, so she can continue her work with joy—that is not mixed with obligation as its foundation.

Using my usual hand gestures and movements, I watch energy release, dissolve, or move out of the client's field. What is happening here is that dissolution is occurring. Because the beliefs and fears bound up in the current challenge are recognized from a different lens, they "no longer matter." The energy that created "what was the matter" is no longer strong enough to hold it together, and it "dis-integrates."

The point of the Reading is for clients to radically shift how they perceive their currently challenging situation and release patterns based on fears that are no longer helpful. By doing this, they reclaim their power so they can make more conscious and creative decisions in their lives.

The stories of past lives/archetypes can also illuminate particular gifts a person possesses, which will be discussed under the inner map's territory in the section called "Essential Gifts."

There is one more aspect to past lives that is relevant in Readings. It is called a "source lifetime." Sometimes several stories on a client's inner map reveal the same theme or dilemma in different historical garb. In that case, after this series of lifetimes with a similar theme is articulated, another kind of story unfolds. This story illuminates the original situation out of which the theme developed—one that sent the client on this path of learning through a particular fear. Because source lifetimes intimately intermingle with the territories inside the invisible map of reality, I will explain more about them in the chapter eleven.

ANCESTRAL PATTERNS

Sometimes a stuck pattern of belief and behavior is fed by an invisible line of ancestral influence. Whether we are diametrically opposed to what is bequeathed us or we are using the ingredients to form a unique blend of learning for this lifetime, as I found in my own heritage, ancestry is an important territory on the invisible map of reality. This point was made clear to me by a client named Israel Antonio, who has given me permission to use his real name.

A gentle man of short, solid stature, with thick black hair and subtle brown highlights came through the door. His body was well toned, his shoulders slightly curved toward his heart. The cane in his hand was not for the sake of his age—he appeared to be in his mid-twenties. He looked at me with only one brown eye; the other was permanently closed. Israel is blind.

He spoke softly, but with clear and deliberate articulation. He told me about a very sad and difficult event in this life. He said that when he was fourteen years old, he woke up one day with a detached retina. Although the doctor thought Israel might recover some ability to see shadows and shapes, that did not happen. Israel was blind in his left eye. From his right eye, he could make out shapes, light, and even perceive colors. After recovering from a long-standing depression, he finally learned to accept his situation—grateful that he could still maintain relative independence.

He decided to attend college and was managing well by his second year. One day he was crossing a street near the university and was hit by a bus. Six years after he went blind in his left eye, and as a result of this accident, Israel lost the sight in his other eye as well. At that moment, he felt the crushing blow of being dependent on others for the rest of his life. He experienced several more years of depression.

As he began to emerge from his inner darkness, he felt pulled to find a way to think about his life differently. A friend of his mentioned my work to him and persuaded him to call.

After we talked about the nature of a Reading, Israel decided to schedule one, and then said, "I think this session is going to change my life."

As a business professional, my first instinct is to manage

expectations. So I said, "Israel, we can be inspired by anything, and often the unexpected. I do hope our session helps you—though it could be the feel of the fabric on the chair you sit in that brings back an inspirational memory. So let's just see what happens."

A few passages from the Gospel came to me as I anticipated Israel's session: "Go and tell John what you have seen and heard: the blind receive their sight, the lame walk, lepers are cleansed..." (Luke 7:22) and "the works that I do, you also shall do; and greater works than these" (John 14:12). At that moment I looked out of the window at the blazing blue sky and thought of another saying: "Anything is possible with God." I said a prayer that I could be a good partner to Spirit in allowing the grace that wanted to love Israel to flow through me for his highest good...and I wondered what might happen!

When the session began and Israel said his name, I immediately Saw a long line of people standing behind him. Their closeness to each other and to Israel indicated that their lives somehow had a deep connection to Israel's path. There was a clear sense that this group was related to Israel—and finally I understood that they were part of his ancestral lineage. Each had, close at hand, images related to a particular aspect of his or her own life. As I articulated some of their stories, I saw a pattern emerge.

"Your ancestors have a pattern woven into their stories that I would call 'downtrodden by circumstances.' They found themselves slaves, servants, peasants, and workers who could earn but meager wages. They humbled themselves, looked at the ground, and accepted their lot. They held close the self-pity that those around them agreed they had a right to feel. After all, what choice did they have but to succumb to life's burdens?

"Your ancestors had a commonly expected response to subjugation. And you have a right to feel the same way as a result of the tragedies in your life. However, your ancestors are hoping you might help them learn something else by the way you respond to your circumstances— circumstances that were foisted upon you and over which you had no control."

Aware of their heartfelt and soul level connection to Israel, I Heard this Biblical phrase as a voice-over: "sins of the father." I define the word "sin" as "actions based on fear." Ultimately, the lessons our souls come to learn are those that Love has not yet transformed from doubt and fear. Whenever we live in fear and choose not to face it, we pass it on—"the unprocessed fears of the father"—to the next generation.

Whenever we choose to do the human homework of looking fear directly in the eye, and feeling the painful results of that act, and staying until peace finds her way to our hearts, we can dedicate that work to our loved ones—even those we haven't met in this life. This is a powerful prayer and intention. And now it was time for Israel to decide about his direction and about his intention.

As I continued to explore Israel's invisible map, I found the question his soul was asking and the core of his life purpose. I expressed it: "Israel, how are you free?

"In what way can you say yes to life? If and however you decide you are free, you will touch those related to you, both genetically and through other relationships, and send them a powerful message. You came to this life to determine this question through a circumstance in which 'no' is more likely and understandable response.

"If you decide you are free and you choose to say yes to life, others will ask, 'How is it possible, given that your situation shows no mercy for the possibility of freedom, that a man who has had such tragic misfortune as losing his sight—twice—can possibly stand up and say yes to life, or can say 'I choose life'?

"The choice is yours, Israel. There is no judgment if you are not yet ready, you cannot feel free, or you decide that saying yes to life is not an option for you. Be honest and authentic with yourself and with the God of your heart. The Universe has infinite patience in your process and will wait until you are ready. What would you like to do?"

As I maintained a heartfelt connection with his whole energy field, it seemed as though the ancestors were watching a baseball game, and the bases were loaded with two outs. It was as if they were holding their collective breath.

Israel paused a moment. Then he said, "I choose life. I want to say yes."

And the batter just hit the ball out of the park. The excitement, relief, and energy released were palpable—as if some lost souls were found, hope was restored, and many could find their place.

After energetically releasing old patterns, belief systems, and related fears, I facilitated a visualization exercise between him and the God of his heart. This exercise sealed his decision and his commitment to fully engage in his life.

At the end of this very powerful session, I asked how he felt. He thought about it for a moment.

"Well, it's good to know that all that has happened to me was not by accident—that there was a reason and a purpose." Then he said, "I'm a playwright and an actor. Some people have encouraged me to write a play about my life, but I couldn't figure out why. Who would want to know about this kind of darkness? Now I know. I'm going to write that play to inspire people. For the rest of my life I want to inspire people."

At that moment, Israel chose to hold his blindness as a tool for grace. By understanding that he had a noble role to play in a world larger than he had ever imagined, he let go of the idea of merely sitting on the sidelines and shutting out the possibilities inherent in life. When Israel's invisible map of reality was brought to light, he was able to make new choices. He changed the organizing principle of his conscious map of reality from despair to inspiration and from fear to love.

As Israel left the office, in answer to my earlier prayer, I clearly Heard Spirit declare:

"And that's how you make a blind man see."

THE SIGHTED SEE WITH NEW EYES

Israel's story continues to inspire. Once he understood his relationship to his ancestors, his personal map expanded. He then felt a new freedom to express his gifts.

His play, "In the Dark," had three successful runs in Chicago, and he has since written and performed four other plays and written two other screenplays.

In addition, he decided to sign up for the New York triathlon, even though he had not been a runner or swimmer when he was sighted. He completed that, and then enlisted in another triathlon, significantly improving his time in all categories. Then he decided to run a marathon, which he finished, and then he did three more, bettering his performance each time.

He is currently talking with producers in Los Angeles about adapting his story for a movie that might encourage others to see their own lives differently.

Israel told me he no longer strives to inspire people. He simply wants to challenge himself to be the best he can be—and if others are inspired, so be it. Israel has chosen to expand his entire map of reality. While at times he has the same self-doubt that we all share, Israel continues to demonstrate the potential of the human spirit.

THE OTHER SIDE

I found I could communicate with those who have passed by accident during a phone call to my father. I mentioned that I was reading about how energy is nonlocal.

"If that's true," I said, "it should be as easy for me to work with people over the phone as it is in person."

"Well, OK," said my dad. "Let me give you someone's name, and you tell me what you See." I felt shy and embarrassed, wondering if I would trip over this opportunity to sound at all sane in front of my beloved and conservative father.

"John Hickman," Dad said.

I waited for an image. "Oh, there he is," I finally said when I could make out his presence. "Well, I See him smiling and waving. He looks happy, and he's playing golf. He says he really likes where he is. That's all I get. Wherever he is, he gets to play golf all the time. Is he on vacation?"

Dad laughed quietly. "That sounds about right. Mr. Hickman was a patient of mine. He loved golf, and he golfed every week of his life…and he died peacefully last week."

I was shocked to learn that I had just contacted someone who has passed!

I slowly began to allow requests for Readings to include contacting those on the Other Side, with many disclaimers as to my inexperience. There were a few challenges. Sometimes I could not Hear a voice, but I would almost See a pantomime, as if the person who crossed over had not yet learned vocal frequency. Sometimes I would get an impression, but it would not be very clear. Interpretation and making meaning turned out to be a process.

Now I understand that meeting someone on their "Other Side" frequency is an art and not a smooth learning curve. There are still times when someone is very easy to Hear and understand, and I can imitate the nuances of his or her manner or voice. Other times the presence is vague and not easily accessible.

In Boulder, I learned that there are different kinds of psychics— those who find missing persons, those who See past lives, and those who tell the future, to name a few. When it comes to communicating with those on the Other Side, it turns out that each medium tunes in differently and accesses different information, which I learned when some client-mediums asked me to help them sort out their work with the Other Side.

One woman clearly Saw the deceased person as if he were standing in the room. She could tell his loved one the color and design of the shirt he wore, and that's all she wanted to do—no messages, just a clear description to let the people who came to her know their loved ones were still with them. Another medium could Hear the deceased but could not See them. She received concrete information, such as where the deceased left the car keys or his will, and would deliver only that information. A few others—both kids and adults—could Feel and Sense spirits and just wanted to know how not to Feel them!

It took some time for me to understand what kind of information comes most readily to me. After a dozen years of blending this communication in with Readings, I have found I am not sensitive to concrete and literal information, though that has come through on occasion. I am tuned in through Hearing and Sensing/Feeling—and on rare occasion Seeing—to soul-level information. This may include the reason the deceased was in a client's life, how he informed and continues to inform the client's life purpose and what he is currently learning after death or how he is helping from the Other Side.

My way of discerning someone's identity comes through a particular rhythm I Hear that is related to their personality, in much the same way as I tune into my "alive" clients. It may be that one spirit is fast and funny, and another is slow and cautious. Each person has a unique rhythm in this life that seems to remain with him or her in the next. I have also Read souls who Feel to me to be so close to the Oneness in the Light that their personalities are hard to distinguish; the brilliance of Love around them is stunning. No matter where a spirit is on that holographic scale, many on the Other Side often indicate to me that they have agreements to stay in contact with their earthbound loved ones until they meet in the Light.

I have listened to those who are in the Light, as well as those who have not "crossed over." I have listened to those who passed from illnesses, died in accidents, were brutally murdered, and those who committed suicide. Through listening in, I have learned a little about what happens in the post-body state. These stories are very intricate, and my clients confirm that whatever I reported to them is how they understood their loved one to be on This Side.

I do not presume to understand what is true about those in the Light. It could be that all souls in the Light are One. Then when a loved one on This Side asks to contact their deceased relative, that relative puts on the robe of his or her former personality for the sake of bringing comfort to my client. It could be that the deceased keep the essence of their personality or particular characteristics through lifetimes, and keep on learning until they remember themselves as wholly beloved and loving.

Perhaps when it is my turn to break through the veil of this life to the next, I shall find a medium through whom I can report back. Until then, these stories are told from the experiences that my clients and I share. Their meaning and conclusion, I leave to you and your imagination.

I tell these stories so you can sense into your own experience of your loved ones who have passed and imagine how they may be unconsciously influencing your map of reality. Awareness allows choice—most especially the choice to be free of the ties that bind you to an unhelpful pattern or past, or the choice to come to peace with the understanding of a loved one's ongoing, invisible love and support.

CROSSING OVER INTO THE LIGHT

At one point many years ago, when I summoned the spirit of a young man whose death circumstances were unknown to me, I found no Light. I looked and looked, but the quality of the energy was heavy. There was no joy, no Lightness of being. I had never experienced this before. Then it simply occurred to me: this young man was not in the Light. He had not yet crossed over. I wasn't sure how to talk about this to my client, Gail, who had been his fiancé. Finally, I simply told her that it did not seem to me that John was in the Light.

Surprisingly, she bowed her head and slumped down. "I was thinking that myself," she said. "His dad told me that he thought the same thing."

"Well, let's see what we can do to encourage him," I said experimentally.

I began imitating John's rhythm to get a sense of him. After a bit, he began to talk—well, he began to babble as he paced. He was talking about how he now understood that he had deeply hurt Gail and his parents. He listed things he should have done, wondering about what he could do about them now. He blurted out his frustration at the finality of his decision. This went on and on.

It was clear that John was a mile-a-minute thinker, which made it challenging to repeat to Gail what he was saying. Finally, I said, "I can barely keep up. He keeps pacing back and forth, talking and talking really fast."

Gail said, "Yes, that's him! He had to pace when he was talking to keep up with his thinking—and he couldn't seem to stop thinking." At this point, Gail explained that John had committed suicide, and now I could understand the context of his musings.

It took a long time and a lot of creative strategy to come up with ideas that might convince John that the Other Side was a good option for him. I realized that a person between worlds has said no to the Light for whatever his reason, and therefore even God's grace is held up until he chooses to open to it. Free will is a powerful gift, and withholding self-forgiveness is, by definition, hell—whether on This Side or the Other.

At one point, I tried explaining to John that there were angels near him, ready to help. I could See them. John said quickly, "I don't believe in angels." I couldn't help but laugh because he said it so fast that he interrupted me in mid-sentence. When I relayed to Gail that I had told John about the angels around him, she interrupted me as quickly as he had, saying, "He doesn't believe in angels."

Even though we were up to serious business, I felt as if I were negotiating the close on a new house for John while he still had eight or nine inspection issues that he felt were unfinished. Finally, Gail talked with him directly, saying that she forgave him, assuring him she would be all right, and telling him she wanted him to go to the Light. I felt John's rhythm slowing down a little, as though he might soon be finished fighting with himself.

Suddenly, I Sensed another presence. It was older, and it felt like a male. As it moved closer, it felt like the presence of a grandparent. I could feel him smiling at John, and I made out that he was holding a pole—perhaps a fishing pole. I Heard him call himself "Papa." I told

John that Papa was waiting for him and wanted to take him fishing.

Gail looked up at me. "John started going fishing with Papa when he was a toddler, and their once-a-year weekend trip was the only time John ever stopped thinking." It was clear that Papa was the draw John needed.

"They have fishing Over There?" he asked as though he were a young boy again.

"Apparently Papa knows all about that," I said. "He's calling you. You'd best go."

He said, "Tell Gail I'll always love her, and thank her for forgiving me." Then he moved toward Papa and blended into the Light. Gail and I looked at each other with wide eyes, as we both experienced a palpable change in the energy in my office.

Since that time, I am clear whether a person is in the Light or has not yet crossed over. Those who have not crossed over are called "ghosts," and those who have reached the Light are called "spirits." Unlike other mediums, I do not See ghosts or spirits on an everyday basis, nor do I walk around talking with them—save those closest to my heart. Understanding now that I have free will, I am clear with those on the Other Side that I am talking with them for the sake of my client's peace in present time—and that they may only come in when I call their name.

SPEAKING OF GHOSTS

I was further educated about ghosts by a book entitled *When Ghosts*

Speak by Mary Winkowski. Ever since she was a child, Ms. Winkowski has been able to See ghosts as clearly as she sees people on This Side. She does not See or communicate with spirits after they go to the Light. Ms. Winkowski's grandmother had the same gift she did, so Ms. Winkowski was able to learn from a well-seasoned medium how to help those who remain between here and the Light to cross over. Her book was used as the basis for the television program Ghost Whisperer, in which James Van Prague, a well-known medium, was executive producer. Since I primarily listen to those in the Light, I found *When Ghosts Speak* and the series Ghost Whisperer to be a helpful education about those in the in-between worlds.

My own interpretation of ghosts is that they are in a place Catholics call "Purgatory" (only this does not seem to be a place of "punishment from above," as Catholics believe). These souls stay in-between worlds, continuing to learn or simply waiting until they can find the desire to be forgiven, forgive themselves, and/or forgive others. I have Seen angels patiently waiting for a person to decide she is willing to receive support and love. Angels are as helpless as God is to rush in and offer help. It is a person's free will that allows or does not.

This is consistent with near-death-experience research across all races, religions, age groups, and both genders. Those interviewed reported that there was no judge waiting for them on the Other Side. Instead, many recalled a "life review," wherein they saw and re-experienced every moment of their lives, which set up its own sense of justice.

Dannion Brinkley is an author and well-known near-death survivor, who has clinically died and come back four times. He says that when he crossed over, he became everyone he had ever encountered, and felt their reactions and feelings toward him. I believe this accounts for why Mr. Brinkley can now be seen hugging everyone he meets.

Those on the Other Side have much to teach us about the heart of life on This Side. The following three stories are examples of this wisdom. I offer these stories because they may enlighten the understanding of our inevitable move into that world and offer us greater peace.

REMEMBERING THE BEST

Sheila died almost a decade before her daughter came for a Reading. Julia still seemed to feel the sting of her mother's death. She was soft-spoken and a bit withdrawn. When she gave me her mother's full name, I Saw a most unusual picture. I kept remembering that Sheila had told me her mother was well into her eighties when she passed, and this image did not fit that description in the least. It also did not match Julia's very short story about her mother.

However, as I am committed to reporting what I See, I said, "Fasten your seatbelt. This is an unusual image. Your mother is wearing a black leather jacket; she is sitting on a motorcycle, and she's saying, 'You've got to ride like the wind! You've got to ride like the wind!'" While I keep my eyes closed when I Read, I hesitantly opened them to see if an offended Julia would leave the room in haste.

I was both relieved and little surprised when I saw a smile on Julia's face. "Yes!" she said. "That was my mother...always the adventurer. She would have gotten on a motorcycle in a hot minute, and said just that!'"

I let out an inner sigh of relief and closed my eyes again to continue. "She says you are very talented, and she wants you to use your talents and enjoy every moment you have. She is saying, 'Life is fleeting, so take risks and learn. Don't be afraid of anything.'"

Julia left saying she felt like she was changed from the inside out. I was so grateful, as I also felt inspired by her mother's presence and encouragement. A month later, I ran into Sandy, a friend of Julia's, who said that Julia was a markedly changed woman since the Reading. Sandy said with a smile that Julia had shared every word of the Reading.

"Oh, yes," I said, "Sheila is a remarkable woman! I loved hearing her wisdom."

"No, not that," Sandy replied.

I was bewildered.

"Oh, that's right," she said, "you didn't know the circumstances."

I shook my head.

"Julia's mother had been sick for eight years before her death. Julia had been at her side the entire time. Because of the long years she spent watching her mother's health deteriorate, Julia forgot what it was like to be with her mother when she was full of life. The Reading reminded her of those good times, and now when she feels sad or depressed, she remembers her mother's words: 'You've got to ride like the wind!'"

COMPASSION RULES FROM THERE TO HERE

My encounter with my next client and her deceased father helped me understand how profoundly the souls who choose to work from the

Other Side can facilitate healing on This Side. When Katie came to see me, I already knew from our brief phone conversation that she had lost her father, Patrick, to a drive-by shooting in an unlikely neighborhood. The police told Katie's family that this had to have been a case of mistaken identity, as Patrick had no ties to gangs and there was no other plausible explanation.

When Patrick came through, I could Feel he was a dear and loving man. He sat down right next to his daughter and put his arm around her. I let her know that, and she smiled. The tears came swiftly.

"The first thing I want to know," she started quietly, as she dabbed her eyes, "is what he wants us to do about the man who shot him. He has not been identified and is still at large." As an only child, Katie felt responsible for doing the right thing. She wanted her dad to know that she and her mom were ready to do anything to bring the shooter to justice. "Does he know who it is? Can he tell us so that the police can catch him? What does he want us to do?" she asked.

I looked at Patrick, listened a moment, and was surprised by his response.

I Heard Patrick say that from the Other Side he knew who the young man was. He also said that he could See that the young man who shot him believed that his mother hated him. Because of that, this young man placed little value on his own life or on others'. He went on to explain that now he had a deep connection to him because of the young man's choice to shoot him—and therefore he had a greater possibility of helping him heal.

I was taken aback at this response.

"Your dad said that whether or not the police catch him is

irrelevant," I translated from what I could discern. "This young man has a spiritual journey through which he will encounter and have to address his choice. In the meantime, your father is hoping he can influence goodness and grace in the young man's life so that he will know and feel he is loved."

From the Light, Patrick knows we are all connected—the wounded, the persecutors, the victims, the saints, and the rescuers. Rather than focus on what human justice would demand—arrest, a trial, incarceration, or death—Patrick said that his moving to the Other Side gave him the precious opportunity to connect with a wounded fellow human being and provide help.

Patrick could clearly see into his killer's mind and heart from the Other Side. He could understand his motivation and the underlying beliefs that led him to violence, and he felt compassion for him. This is the essence of a spiritual response to a human situation. Patrick had the power to forgive his assailant—and he had.

When someone has been wronged or violated, he is a victim with every right to both feel and act out of rage, anger, and revenge. If instead he chooses to use his power to forgive, he and the receiver of that forgiveness are forever changed by mercy and compassion.

This does not mean that perpetrators are released from accountability for their harmful actions. But the one who suffered the offense has the unique power to ask Spirit to release the other person from any spiritual debt incurred on his behalf. To be on the receiving end of mercy, if it is accepted, is humbling and positively life changing. Patrick hoped that one day the young man who shot him would know that experience.

I wondered if Katie would be disappointed with Patrick's response, given her desire to assure justice for her father.

Instead, Katie said, "That is just like my father! He was a coach at the local high school. Everyone loved him. He would put the kids who were having the hardest time under his wing as though they were special and spend the most time with them."

Patrick's compassionate heart remained unchanged on the Other Side.

Then Patrick continued in an unexpected direction. He began to describe the placement of furniture in their family room. I relayed what I Heard to Katie. "Your dad is telling me that in the family room, the couch is pushed against a back wall and that there is an afghan lying across the top of it. He's showing me that next to the couch is a treadmill, and that the television is in front of it."

As I described this, Katie said, "Yes, that's exactly what the family room looks like."

Then Patrick said, "Tell Katie that this is what it is like to die: When we're alive, we run on the treadmill—and while we keep running and running, we watch the television in front of us. Then we change the channel as we continue to run, and then change it again and again. Finally, we turn off the television, step off the treadmill…and there we are. Just ourselves…

"And that's what it's like to be dead."

I Heard Katie inhale.

Then Patrick said, "Tell Katie that when she misses me, she should sit on the couch and wrap the afghan around her. Those will be my arms around her, holding her."

When I opened my eyes, Katie was smiling with tears running down her face. She said, "My father and I used to sit on that couch in the evening and watch television together, with the afghan wrapped around both of us."

Patrick's words reminded me that each person is doing the best he can in this life, with the gifts and the wounds he bears. There are many in the Light, whom I've had the privilege to Read, who seek opportunities to help and heal those still on Earth. They very much want us to understand that, even when we can't feel it, we are beloved and always in connection with the Divine.

HELPING EACH OTHER THROUGH LIFETIMES

A petite, dark-haired beauty walked into my office.

"Hi, Delia," I said. "What can I do for you today?"

Delia could not get a word out before tears welled up in her eyes. It took some time for her to regain her composure. "My son was born prematurely. He was alive for a little while, and then he died." She stopped again to cry. Given the depth of her grief, I assumed this was very recent event.

Instead, Delia said, "It has been over two years, and I cannot stop grieving. When he was born, the doctors implied there were extraordinary things they could do to keep him alive. It was so risky we decided not to put him through it. We let him go, and now I blame myself. Maybe there was something I could have done and he would be with me now. I have four other children who need me, and I can't be there for them the way they deserve."

"Did you name your son?" I asked.

"Yes, his name was Samuel," she replied, as the tears began anew.

I closed my eyes and asked Delia to say her full name three times. As she finished, an image appeared of a very large, lovely house with a porch that wrapped all the way around it. It was surrounded by green fields. Delia turned into one of the two women sitting on the porch.

She was the larger of the two women, with a loud, boisterous voice that boomed with pride as she spoke about her eight children. She was having summer tea with a neighbor.

"I dare say," said Delia, with an instructor's tone, "children should be free to run around and explore life. It's what takes the devil out of them so they and we can sleep well at night." Her neighbor smiled politely and with some reserve, as this theory of childrearing was not widely shared. It was a time when people had recently stopped fiercely believing that children should be seen and not heard.

"Look at them," Delia continued proudly, pointing to three of her children in view. "They are full of life. They are happy and healthy. I tell you, this is the way families will raise their children in the future."

Just then there was a shout from what seemed a long way away.

Delia laughed. "They let out their energy through their ample vocal chords too, don't they?"

Another shout followed, and this time it was closer. She could finally make out the words. "Coyote attack! Mabel, Jon, Martha, Timmy. Help!" It was a breathless, anguished cry from one of Delia's older children.

Delia bolted out of her seat and ran—faster than seemed possible for her substantial frame. When she finally reached her children, there was blood everywhere. Three of her children's bodies crumpled together, as though they had fought a united battle and lost.

"Before this moment, you were wide open to life and its possibilities for you and your children," I commented. "After this tragedy, you were understandably closed down, and blamed yourself for the death of your children.

"In the next lifetime, you were secretly, quietly working with another man, Amos, shepherding families and orphaned children over enemy lines toward the possibility of safety in refugee camps. You were oblivious to your personal risk and hardly slept or ate so that you could keep an eagle eye on the travelers. While literally hundreds of families were saved through your efforts, there were several children who, having gotten lost, you found lying dead in the grass.

"You were inconsolable," I continued. "Amos put his arm around you and pointed toward the families who were safely on the other side. 'They are free because of you,' he said. 'In all this tragedy, there are bound to be those whom our Father in Heaven chooses to bring Home.'" Amos was at peace with the situation, knowing some would make it and some would not. In his view, some families traveled over the border to a new life on Earth, and others traveled over the border to new life in Heaven.

"You could not hear Amos in the midst of your grief," I said. Then another picture began to move on her left side, and I turned my attention in that direction.

"Well, now," I said, interrupting my own story of Delia and Amos. "Here is a lifetime with a different feel to it. In this story, you were a very gifted, young, bold dance teacher, who had her own studio. You wanted to demonstrate and teach the kind of dance you felt everyone should embody. You taught your students that dance is a dynamic balance of 'open and close, in and out, expansion and contraction.'

"'When you express one side of this pair,' you instructed, 'it's opposite calls for expression so that the whole can be celebrated through the dance of life. When you are too open and cannot contract, you are not reflecting and integrating what you learned by engaging life. When you are too frightened to open, the gift of your dance cannot be known.'

"Some students could express this dynamic balance," I continued, "and some could not. You converted a large closet area that was attached to your dance studio into a room of mirrors. When someone could not demonstrate balance, you sent him or her to this room for reflection.

'Go reflect on your life and find out how you are stuck. Discover a way to express the opposite of that which comes most easily to you. Then come back and begin again the dance of life.' For some students, a period of reflection would result in new steps and flexibility. Others would return, still feeling defeated in their efforts to open.

"You were strict and clearly judgmental," I related, "the kind of judgment that can only be expressed by someone inexperienced in life, and in her mid-twenties. If students could not find new steps to their dance after repeated periods of reflection (and with no other coaching), you asked them to leave your dance company." I watched as time seemed to speed up, and other elements appeared in the scene.

"It was not until you lost your beloved twin in an accident ten years later that you, yourself, could not find a way to open. Compassion for others was born in you then.

"Now," I said, returning to present time, "please give me your baby's name."

As Delia tearfully and quietly said, "Samuel Nathan Beecher," I Saw a beautiful, tall, male spirit standing just next to her.

I asked her to say her name with his. Upon hearing them together, I Saw the spirit move into the character of Amos.

"He was Amos, Delia. He understood the cycle of life and that 'there is no death.' He was so sad that you could not embrace this understanding; he has come back to help you.

"I know it is an odd thing to say that he is here to help you, when his presence and departure brought you such pain," I continued. "However, when you have a long-held, self-defeating belief, you bring the same feelings associated with those beliefs back through an experience in this life—not the exact experience as in other lifetimes, but in the same theme.

In this case, it is the tragic loss of a child for which you blame yourself. When the intense feelings return, you have an opportunity with your free will to make another choice than the one you made in other lifetimes, which was to shut down and self-condemn.

"Your experience with Samuel held the elements of your deepest fear-based belief from these other lives. The way you can tell that you are working on the resolution of a fear-based belief is that a part of you knows your response to a situation is out of proportion. In this case, you said that after two years since Samuel passed, the intensity of your grief has not diminished." I turned back then to the tall spirit, now standing in front of Delia with his arm outstretched, as if he were asking her for the next dance.

"Samuel says he wants to be *your* dance teacher now. He wants you to reclaim the openness you left behind in the lifetime where you had eight children. 'The dynamic balance of the dance of life requires that of you,' he is saying with some humor as he imitates the strict, knowing voice you used as a twenty-something dance instructor. He says you will know it is him when you see mirrors and dance."

Then Samuel slipped into the image of the smiling baby boy he was two years ago for a very brief time. "Samuel says, 'I got to smile; then I left.'" I could Feel his joy as he remembered the act of smiling through his little body.

At that point, Delia agreed to participate in a visualization wherein she looked deeply into the hearts of all the characters she had played in the other lifetimes, and asked for and allowed forgiveness. When I asked whether she was able to complete this exercise, she said, "Almost. I'm OK."

I requested that she gather all parts of herself for which she could not find forgiveness and put them in a basket. Then I asked her to give the basket to the Divine Mother, whose all-encompassing compassion would do the rest for her.

When Delia felt complete, she opened her tear-filled eyes.

"I have to tell you this," she said. "I just finished installing mirrors all over my house so I can dance. I love to dance." She paused a moment and then added, "And Samuel did open his eyes—and he smiled. And then he died." Then she smiled, too. "I feel lighter," she said.

THE SPECIAL CASE OF SUICIDE

While it is good to remember that we are connected to Light, many clients, such as Gail in the first story, have a keen sense that their loved one is not in the Light. Also, some clients are afraid for loved ones who have taken their own lives because they were taught that suicide is a serious sin.

Since, as I said, I define "sin" as "an action based on fear," then suicide may be a "sin." However, I have learned from many whom I have contacted on the Other Side that when we act based on fear, even though we are giving up on ourselves, Spirit never gives up on us— ever. The three stories below revealed to me the infinite patience of the Divine, waiting with open heart and grace for the moment we choose to release self-condemnation.

I offer these stories because suicide can be a sustaining pain and heavy influence on our sense of choice. Once the stories of those who have taken their own lives are revealed, it may assist those who have had a loved one leave this way to find peace.

WHEN HELP COMES TOO LATE

Marcy was a reluctant client, referred to me by someone who was very concerned about her well-being. It had been two years since her daughter had died, and she still went home every day after work and could barely move. Marcy said she did not believe in what I did, but at this point she was desperate. Since she lived a distance away, we did the

Reading over the phone.

"Jessica was only twenty-one years old," Marcy said. "She was my only child. After my divorce, it was just Jessica and me for many years. When she graduated from college, she searched for a while and finally found a job. I knew it was stressful and didn't pay well, but the job allowed her to be on her own, which she really wanted. She found a small but nice apartment. We talked a couple of times a week. After only a few months, I knew that she felt overwhelmed."

It was Christmas Eve when Jessica called from her apartment, hysterical. "Mom!" she cried frantically. "I took too many sleeping pills! I don't want to die! Please help me, please!" Marcy was stunned, but she found the focus to immediately call 911. When the paramedics arrived, it was too late. It was a parent's worst nightmare.

As Marcy said Jessica's name, I Saw Jessica in an ethereal, gray place. There seemed to be little direct light, but there was open space where Jessica slowly and thoughtfully strolled back and forth as though she were calculating or recalling something. There were angels lined up as though they were the wallpaper of Jessica's gray place. Each angel was busy with some small task like stitching or meditating. I had a sense that they had infinite patience and were simply respecting Jessica's timing.

"Marcy," I began, "Jessica is very focused on figuring out what happened and how she feels about different aspects of her actions. She is not accepting the help that is all around her. There are angels lined up to assist, waiting for her to request help. However, Jessica wants to work out the problems by herself—she is insistent. She wants to find her own answers.

"I have a sense that she is determined and she will find her way. Jessica is protected as she is pondering. Whenever she decides she has found the answers she is looking for, the angels will be there for her."

This was not a case of moving Jessica into the Light. She was simply not open to assistance—angels' or mine. However, neither was there a sense that she was stuck or depressed, nor that she would stay in this state for very much longer.

I could hear Marcy crying. Then she laughed through her tears: "That is just how Jessica did everything—she always wanted to work things out for herself, and she wouldn't let anyone else help her. I had to insist to accompany her to find her first apartment."

As I described a little more of what I Saw, Marcy felt sure that I was talking about Jessica, her baby girl. It brought her comfort to know her daughter was not in a terrible place and that eventually, she would move on, surrounded by the help she might eventually want.

Then I turned my attention to Marcy. I could see that her self-esteem was low—a condition that had preceded her daughter's situation. Marcy was not aware of her many gifts and did not honor herself or her contribution as important. Facilitating healing for her so that she could feel more sure-footed moving forward, we closed the Reading, and Marcy said she felt more at peace.

Three months later I got a letter from Marcy saying that she finally felt stronger. She said that after her divorce years ago, she chose not to purchase her house. She knew she didn't have the self-confidence to take care of it. Rather, she rented a small apartment for Jessica and herself.

In the past month, she made the decision to move out of her

apartment and buy a home for herself. She also said she was able to be more fully present in her teaching job at the high school. Marcy said she was still sad now and then, but the sadness was not debilitating as it had been. She felt lighter.

The last remarks in the letter were these: "I still don't understand what you do, but I know it has helped me. I teach English, and every year we study Shakespeare and his play Hamlet. Now, when I hear the line from Hamlet 'There is more to life, Horatio, than what you read in your philosophy books,' I will think of you and how you helped me find Jessica."

There is no greater tragedy in life than for parents to bury their child. Worse still is when that child has taken her own life. The kaleidoscope of emotions and the unending self-judgment are daily trials.

In the next story, Bonnie, who gave me permission to use her real name, came to me to contact her beautiful, successful, popular daughter who was now on the Other Side. Bonnie did not tell me how she had died…that I found out from her daughter.

A DAUGHTER'S PURPOSE FROM THE OTHER SIDE

Bonnie's big blue eyes looked at me with great sadness and sincerity. She said, "Hilary told me to come to you." I asked what she meant. "My daughter, Hilary, died two years ago. She sends me signs—hearts and keys. I saw this…" and she handed me a key with a heart carved into the bottom of it. "And she told me you have the key."

As convinced as I am that those on the Other Side sends signs and signals to loved ones, I felt a bit intimidated, as I'd never met Bonnie. What key could I possibly have for her? If it was about what Hilary wanted to say to Bonnie in a Reading, what if I couldn't Hear what Hilary was saying, as happens on occasion? What if I didn't accurately convey Hilary's meaning and Bonnie felt worse when she left? I couldn't bear to think of adding to the pain of a parent who had lost her child.

"I typically do not receive earthbound information, such as where someone left her diary or her favorite jacket," I explained, trying to manage Bonnie's expectations and my own trepidation. "There are mediums who Read exclusively at that level. I Read soul-level information, offering you a higher level understanding of your relationship with Hilary." I almost hoped she would ask me for the contact information for another kind of medium.

Instead, Bonnie said she understood, and the anticipation in her face did not change. She said her daughter was sixteen years old when she passed over. I still felt a bit concerned about whether I could satisfy whatever other expectations I sensed that Bonnie was not sharing. Nevertheless, I said a prayer; then Bonnie said Hilary's name, and I called to her from my heart.

The very first impression I got was a happy girl who was saying, "Mahahahm" in long tones as she tilted her head, mocking a sassy expression. Again, given what I thought Bonnie might be hoping for—a meaningful conversation with her daughter—this wasn't exactly an appropriate prelude.

However, I took the risk as I always do and said, "OK, Bonnie, this is what I'm Seeing and Hearing…" and I imitated Hilary's stance, attitude, and word.

Bonnie laughed. "That's her!" she said. "That's Hilary!"

I sighed one big breath. Later Bonnie told me that as she was driving to the Reading, she talked with Hilary, as she often does. Bonnie told Hilary that she would know it was she who came through if she heard just that expression and the "Mahahahm" that was so familiar to Bonnie.

Hilary was an unusual case. She seemed happy—a beautiful spirit, bouncing up and down, doing flips and jumps. As I relayed this to Bonnie, she told me Hilary was a cheerleader. She seemed to have much to say as she continued to bounce…until Bonnie asked me this question: "Ask her why she had to die that way."

Suddenly, Hilary stopped moving, and it seemed as if this were the first time she had thought about her own death. I was waiting for her response when the image moved to a visual that was very dark, and I immediately felt like I was choking. This was entirely uncharacteristic, as I am not the kind of medium where others' experiences overtake me. I typically receive a narrative of events, images, and stories. I can touch into feelings and describe them, but after decades of practice, I allow the feelings of others to stay with them.

However, the choking feeling went on for a bit, and then vertigo overtook me, as I felt I was with Hilary, re-experiencing her death.

It felt as though Hilary was clinging to me in much the same way as my own daughter clutched onto me when she was three years old and something frightened her. There was much confusion, and I did not know what was happening—only that I was caught in something over which I had no control. I could sense Hilary was trying to sort through all these feelings for herself.

As if she suddenly and for the first time understood what happened when she passed, Hilary began to cry hysterically. Bonnie was aware something had gone wrong when I began to cough. She asked if I was OK.

I said, "Yes, I think Hilary is just processing what she went through at the end." Hilary was crying, "Mommy, Mommy, I'm so sorry. I am so sorry!"

It was also the first time Hilary had felt the impact she had had on her mother and her family. I let her mother know that Hilary was sorry.

Bonnie's sweet mothering quickly emerged as she said, "Honey, it's OK. I know it was confusing. I love you. I'll always love you!"

I Saw Hilary sit down and weep.

Bonnie continued, "I just want to know you are all right, sweetie. I just want to know that you are going to be OK."

Hilary's sadness finally lightened, and she went over to her mother and put her arm around her. Bonnie closed her eyes and tears came, as though she could feel her daughter's presence.

Bonnie had not been oriented toward energy, spirits, or communicating with those on the Other Side before Hilary's passing. Now she was exploring whatever avenue she could to assure herself that Hilary was safe. Parents who have children who take their own lives are on the very bottom of the crucible of life—having to turn to their strong faith, find some light that helps them go on, or find new ways to understand their situation.

In any case, it is a daily emotional struggle that mixes self-condemnation with exquisitely painful concern for their child—

especially if they have been told that suicide is a serious sin, with punishment attached.

In Bonnie's case, she sought out signs her daughter was still with her. In addition, Hilary began to tell me how she wanted to work with her mother to assure more teens did not die as she had. At times, Hilary gave very specific instructions for her mother's consideration.

Later, Bonnie revealed that Hilary had died by hanging herself.

Bonnie had to move through much grief after our Reading, and many months passed before she was actually able to receive the "action items" Hilary had laid out for her. Finally, in her determination to fulfill her daughter's wishes, Bonnie started an organization called Hillary's Hope to help prevent teen suicide. She has given talks at high schools where one hundred teens listen and cry as they hear not only about Hilary's story, but how to recognize the signs of depression and what they can do for themselves or their friends.

Bonnie also discovered that her other eleven-year-old daughter, Kendall, who was diagnosed with a disorder, is able to See and discern Hilary's spirit as well as other spirits. Bonnie had begun nurturing her gifts and encouraged her to write her own story of grief to help other children her age, which is now published. Kendall has also spoken to student-filled auditoriums about how she dealt and continues to deal with her sister's passing.

In addition, Bonnie has begun to train in energy work. She said some day perhaps she will be able to offer her healing work to parents who have lost children to suicide. What is astonishing is how Bonnie's courage, determination, and self-awareness have changed the worst possible situation a parent can bear into a blessing for many. There is no doubt that when I now contact Hilary, she is dedicated to working in partnership with her mother to positively influence as many teens as she can who are in jeopardy of ultimate despair.

Bonnie's evolution in spirit does not mean there is an absence of days where she can barely get out of bed from missing Hilary, or that she never feels anxiety. The more Bonnie practices, the stronger her spiritual tools become—so that when the devastating emotions arise, she can apply them or know to whom she can reach out when life feels overwhelming.

Bonnie's character has grown considerably since she chose to look her grief in the face and move forward with her life. Hilary is also growing in spirit on the Other Side.

CONTINUING EDUCATION ON THE OTHER SIDE

Aikeko was a petite, almost frail-looking Asian woman, with a neatly arranged scarf on a beautifully appointed ensemble. It was clear that detail was important to her. She sat at the edge of my office couch and softly told me the story of her mother's passing.

Her mother, Yoshiko, had never traveled outside the small village in which she, her mother, and her grandmother were born. She was married very young, had four children, and tried to be a good wife and mother. Aikeko's father died a year before her plans to move to California to be educated in the United States. Her two younger brothers were both away at school, and her older sister, Kaya, had moved home to attend to her mother. Kaya convinced Aikeko that she should follow her plans to go to the States, and that she would take good care of their mother.

Aikeko wrote home often about her experiences in California, and visited her family in Japan every other year, when her finances allowed. Several years after she moved away, Aikeko sensed from her sister's letters that her mother was depressed. While Aikeko tried to talk with her sister about this situation, Kaya dismissed it, saying everything would be fine. She convinced Aikeko to concentrate on her new and important position at a bank, and encouraged her to do well. And so she did.

One day Aikeko received a phone call from her bereft sister, telling her that their mother had taken her own life.

This happened three years prior to the day Aikeko arrived in my office. "Where is my mother?" she asked me. "Is she OK? Is she in a difficult place?"

I asked Aikeko to say her mother's full name, and then I waited to see what would happen. After a moment or two of silence, I perceived a very small-framed woman appear near the ceiling of my office. She stopped and bowed, seeming to ask permission to enter. Certainly that was a first in my experience with those on the Other Side. I bowed in return, indicating that it would be an honor for me to have her in my home. This response came from a part of me already beginning to be in rapport with Yoshiko's energy.

As she came in, Yoshiko smiled a humble half-smile at her daughter, and immediately I felt pride gently flow from her heart. I silently asked how she was doing, and she gestured backward toward the portal through which she had entered.

I looked there and Saw a small, sweet home that she indicated belonged to her. Yoshiko allowed me to look into her simple abode, and then she opened the back door to reveal a tiny garden that was as beautifully landscaped as are Japan's finest urban meditation gardens.

She waved toward the meditation cushion that sat in the middle of her fragrant flowers. It was well worn. Bringing my attention back inside the house, Yoshiko showed me many large canvases—side by side.

I described all this to Aikeko as she silently continued to listen. "Below the canvases are inkwells and paint brushes," I said to Aikeko. "She is practicing calligraphy."

I wondered what she was painting.

Just then, she reenacted the scene moments before her passing—using the metaphor of pulling a cover over her whole body to demonstrate how completely alone she felt. As I watched her disappear underneath that bulky blanket, the feeling became tragically sad.

"Your mother picked up the brush and is applying the ink," I said after describing to Aikeko her mother's sorrow. "She is painting a new Japanese character on the canvas—one she invented—to represent those feelings of isolation and sadness she experienced in her final moments on Earth."

Then I watched as Yoshiko tried to imagine how another kind of response to her situation might have felt. It was as though she were "trying on" other emotions to explore other conclusions.

"Your mother is trying to sense what other kinds of feelings were possible at the last moments of her life. With each new imagining, her expression is changing. After she reenacts each possibility, she stands up and paints a new Japanese character on another canvas."

Then something extraordinary occurred: "Your mother is painting a new character that combines the reaction she actually had in her last moments, with these others she has 'tried on.'"

As she painted, Yoshiko indicated to me that Japanese consciousness had a special ability to allow and hold paradox without conflict.

What the Western mind thinks of as opposite, the Eastern mind can hold as complimentary or paradoxical, such as the Japanese symbol for "crisis," which is the same as the character for "opportunity." Instead of opposing each other, the Japanese see that within every crisis is a new opportunity. This is also like the Tao symbol. Masculine and feminine may be opposite to the Western mind, but in Asia, the Tao represents the two separate energies being held in one whole circle.

This is what Yoshiko was trying to discern for herself and her life—what paradox could she hold about the life she just lived? What could she learn about the possibilities that existed within the tragic response she had?

Then a most wondrous movement occurred: Yoshiko stood behind the canvas upon which she had painted the paradoxical character, and walked into it…

I heard Yoshiko speak for the first time. "In my next life, I will be embodying 'this character' I am becoming."

Aikeko cried quietly as I described her mother's elegant response to her life, her learning, and her next steps. She said, "I am so glad my mother has found her way. I was so concerned for her and how she must have felt when she died. I wished I could have been there with her and my sister. I wondered if I could have prevented this or made a difference in her decision."

This is a question so many loved ones ask concerning someone who has taken their own life: "Could I have saved my loved one?"

What I know from communicating with those on the Other Side who have taken their lives is that they blame no one but themselves. Even if much of the fuel for their decision came from others or another, most of those who are in between worlds realize that they made a choice, and now they ponder the consequences in the context of an environment that supports their learning.

There are those whose self-hatred causes them to avoid the Light offered on the Other Side. And so it is helpful to remember that at all times our prayers and intentions find their mark if the person on the Other Side is open to support. Indeed it is helpful to "pray unceasingly" for others. We need each other and loving intention—on This Side and the Other Side.

Yoshiko showed me the richness of life beyond this one. Perhaps her willingness to share her generous revelation can expand our map of reality concerning what happens to our loved ones following suicide.

Despite having taken her own life, Yoshiko showed that learning continues, without judgment or punishment. In fact, Yoshiko had at her disposal all the resources and support that made her self-exploration comfortable and intimate. Her story helps us to take a deep breath before self-judgment limits our thinking about possibilities, and helps us remember that this is an eternal journey, accompanied by unending support and love.

Aikeko said, "Thank you. Tonight I will sleep in peace."

REFLECTION

Those in the Light know mercy and compassion and do not seek justice in the sense that we understand it from This Side of the veil. Those who have not yet stepped into the Light withhold forgiveness—from themselves or others—and can be helped and sometimes persuaded by those on This Side to move toward the Love that awaits them. Perhaps I have learned the most from those who have committed suicide.

The suicide of a loved one is perhaps the single most impactful event on our reality. The heartbreak is unfathomable. When it is understood that, even well after suicide, hope and love remain a kinetic potential, greater peace is possible. It may even allow those who remain on This Side to take up their lives again.

CHAPTER ELEVEN

Territories within the Invisible Map

This chapter explores the five interconnected territories on the invisible map of reality: essential gifts, fear-based beliefs, persistent challenges/soul lessons, life purpose, and destiny points. Using clients' stories, I explore each of these separately, and then their interconnectedness is illuminated.

ESSENTIAL GIFTS

As a teenager, it was clear to me that my brothers and sisters had distinct talents and gifts. Even as young children, many of my siblings showed a proclivity toward one distinct area or another. My sister, Mary, used to doodle while talking on the phone. When she hung up, the doodle was an identifiable cartoon character. Today it is very hard to distinguish whether her final work is a painting or a photograph.

My younger brother, Ed, used his precise and laser-like mind to determine which tools would make things work and how things fit together. Today he is a brilliant nuclear and environmental engineer. Another sister, Laura, at the age of eleven, stayed inside most of the summer, letting us know she was typing her first novel. Today she is an extraordinary journalist, author, editor, and teacher. The list of talented siblings goes on and on. When I was just beginning my high-school years and thought about my own gifts, I came up empty.

The only passion I could identify was my desire to be a priest. Given the Church's stand on a men-only priesthood, which created the greatest confusion of my life, I looked around at related choices. Many people encouraged the convent as a viable alternative for Catholic women who were spiritually inclined. The paradigm of women obediently taking orders from men was on its last legs in the seventies and eighties, and I had no desire to bow to masculine authority as a rule.

Therefore, one day I prayed, "Please, God, tell me what I am good at so I will know how to focus my attention, and then I'll know what to do when I grow up. What am I good at?" I opened my heart wide to receive the response.

Here is what I Heard: "You are good at praying for people."

"Praying for people?!" I can't tell you how anticlimactic that response felt.

"OK, yes," I resentfully and silently replied, "I do pray and maybe even well, but how in the world am I going to make a living by praying for people? No college courses support that gift!" For many years I was disappointed and dismayed by this clear response.

As I now look back over a few decades since that incident, I think about the thousands of Readings I've given and the business leaders with whom I've consulted. I always begin with a prayer, sometimes silently, sometimes aloud, but always with a prayer that the highest good will be done for every person present, for the matter we came together to address, and/or for the spirit of the company and its workers. I consider every consulting engagement a call from the leader's soul and every Reading a deep prayer for a person's well-being.

Perhaps my strongest gifts are prayer-powered work and naming other people's gifts.

Identifying, articulating, and honoring others' gifts became even more important as I began to See patterns in clients' energy fields. I call them "essential gifts" because they seem to be at the very core of someone's identity. They are proclivities that are available from birth, and easily cultivated. They are orientations or even skills that come so easily to us that we often do not name them as gifts because they seem "perfectly normal" to us.

These unique gifts are very subtle. For example, one client, Danielle, who was an attractive, petite, blond woman, said she felt stuck in her career direction. She did not tell me what she did. When she said her name, here's what came to me:

"In another life, you were a very big, rotund Italian man who owned a little restaurant in the middle of a small village. Oddly, you did not especially like to cook. The food you served customers was so-so, but your heart was enormous. People loved you and wanted to be in your company. You wanted the villagers to come together and tell each other stories because you believed that's how people really got fed. Your restaurant became 'the heart of the town.'

"You are not interested in providing a place where people come to solve their problems or find a spot to work. Your essential gift is to know how to create a space and environment where people find joy in being together."

Danielle laughed out loud. "It's so true. I have dinner parties nearly every weekend, but I make everyone else cook. Then I make everyone tell stories about the funniest or weirdest thing that's happened to them since the last time we met. I've even been thinking about someday buying my own restaurant. Then I think, 'Why would I want to do that when I don't like the food part?!' Now I get it."

Danielle is now aware that her essential gift is to "feed everyone" by creating joyful community, so she can build a future on her true strengths. When we build our lives this way, we are doing the work we came to do.

One other important part of essential gifts is that they are also used defensively to cover fears. For example, if you are exquisitely sensitive to others' needs, and you do not believe you deserve to receive care, few others will question you about that.

Instead, you will likely receive many compliments about and emotional rewards for your caregiving that help you keep your defenses strong and your sadness and fear well hidden in your invisible map. In so many cases we do not realize that our motivation is fueled by fear rather than love. It is important to know that essential gifts have two sides and to be aware of how we employ them.

Sometimes specific qualities, such as independence and loyalty, are glued to essential gifts and appear as a motif through many life challenges. For example, Marianne was extremely loyal to her loved ones, and as she talked, it was apparent that they took priority over any of her own interests and desires. She smiled as she talked about the ways she could multitask on behalf of the multiple demands on her from her siblings and parents.

Marianne said, "I don't really need anything. I'm just happy taking care of others."

When prompted to talk more about her own needs, Marianne said she didn't really have any desires she could think of for herself. And she felt guilty and selfish whenever she tried.

In her Reading, Marianne had a lifetime where she rejected any responsibility for her powerful family's political position as well as the consequences of her falling in love and marrying a member of the opposing tribe. When her family of origin was later killed by her husband's family, Marianne felt ashamed that she had valued her independence over family loyalty.

In this life, she cares for her now-adult siblings as if they are her children. She also fears, in her hidden core, that if she is not loyal, others will die and the blood will be on her hands. In addition, since she fulfilled her desires in love in that lifetime, and that equated to her family's death, her unconscious mind believes it is dangerous for her even to formulate desires for herself, much less fulfill them.

So in this case, her essential gift of caregiving is defined and shaped by the qualities of independence and loyalty that seem to be juxtaposed. Part of Marianne's life lesson, as will be further explained in the subchapter on *Fear-Based Beliefs, Soul Lessons, and Source Lifetimes,* is to collapse the polarity of loyalty and independence into a paradox.

That is, until Marianne grounds her loyalty in her own heart's desire and forgives herself, she will continue to find persistent life challenges regarding these qualities. She will also remain confused as to why her actions based on loyalty feel empty and obligatory, and sometimes produce resentment.

PERSISTENT CHALLENGES

When my brother, Gene, begins a conversation about the auditing and accounting problems he encounters at work, I immediately picture the image I used to regularly see in one of my college classes: a frog on a computer screen holding a banner that said, "Plato is about to Croak," just before the monitor went blank. This happened in an accounting course in one of the first computerized learning environments—when systems bugs often caused all the connected terminals to lose the hard work of their users.

Accounting was the only course in which I could not earn a good grade. The detail involved in balancing numbers into a meaningful outcome has been a persistent challenge for me throughout my life. However, this is not the kind of persistent challenge that is a territory on our invisible maps of reality.

Rather, the persistent challenges that merit a place on the landscape of our hidden maps are those that infiltrate both personal and professional aspects of our lives and hold secret yearnings, such as the loyalty and independence that Marianne's story illustrates. These challenges persist despite therapy, "change your life" programs, and even intuitive Readings. However, as the next story illustrates, they can become guides for our deepest growth in spirit.

Walking to the reception desk after having finished an intuitive

Reading, I asked my assistant the name of the next client (who has given me permission to use her real name here) Jasmin replied, "Jenniffer." I asked, "Jenniffer who?" She said, "I don't know, she wouldn't give me her last name." She and I exchanged looks, and then we burst out laughing. That was a first. "Do you think she's a movie star or a criminal?" I asked. Jasmin replied, "You're the intuitive. Look it up!"

When "Just Jenniffer" walked in, I did not recognize her—though I'm hardly one to keep current on the stars—and I checked for weapons. Jenniffer asked me about the nature of a Reading, and I gave her my practiced reply. Then she asked, "What about the 'talking to the dead people' part?"

Frustrated that the label "medium" had recently been applied to me as my main work, I said in haste, "I am not a phone line to the dead. If it is important to bring you to peace, then I will contact someone on the Other Side. Otherwise, my work is to help you—the living person—to find your power and your peace."

Jenniffer thought about this for a moment, and then said, "Well, I think I'd like to make a career change, and I'm not sure what to do."

"OK then," I responded with relief. "Let's get started." I recited the prayer I always say before starting the Reading, and then said, "If I have permission to Read your energy, would you please give me your full name three times?"

When she was quiet for longer than is typical, I opened my eyes for a moment and noticed that she seemed disappointed. Then I remembered that she had withheld her last name. Finally, when Jenniffer said her full name, I was sure I'd never heard it before and remained baffled as to her motive for seeking anonymity. I chalked it up to a quirky personality and continued.

The stories on Jenniffer's energy field started with an image of two men. "There are two men here in your third chakra—the area where information about your power, control, role, and responsibility are located. One man is tall, the other short. I'm Seeing you with the tall man and here is the story: you are a Quaker woman, washing, cooking, cleaning, and this man is not appreciating you or your work. No matter how hard you try to prove your love for him, he largely ignores you."

Another image popped up just behind that one. "Here is another story. It looks like in another lifetime. You worked as this man's speechwriter when he was an orator in Rome. The speeches are astounding successes. You receive neither recognition nor appreciation for your efforts." More stories followed.

The persistent challenge that emerged for Jenniffer, regardless of the century, was that she gave away her power to those she considered to have greater authority than her. She sought to please and gain approval, recognition, and praise from others. Yet she remained unrecognized and unfulfilled.

Jenniffer later acknowledged that she currently had two bosses, one taller than the other. She said she "worked like a dog" to get noticed by the taller one, and "minus the Quaker outfit" she felt exactly as I had described.

About an hour into the Reading, I said, "Jenniffer, there is a man here who looks like he's in his mid-fifties, and he seems very excited to be here. He's jumping up and down and showing me X's and O's on a board. Now he's talking about games and moves." At first it looked to me like he was referring to a game of tic-tac-toe. Then I got the impression that he was referring to sports games. I said, "This man is talking about sports…oh, he says he is your father."

I didn't know if Jenniffer's father had passed away, but through this image, it felt as if he were communicating from the Other Side. It is not typical in Readings that a person who has passed over simply "pops through." If my client is emotionally unfinished with someone on the Other Side, I ask her to say that person's full name, and then I "call him in."

"Jenniffer," I said, "your father" (I did not know his name) "is saying that he is proud of you. Now, from the Other Side, he understands why you were unhappy in your job. He's saying that he knows he convinced you to stay in your current job because he thought it would bring you security for the future. But from where he stands now, he can see that what he identified as important is, in fact, not significant from an eternal perspective."

Jennifer's father went on for some time, at one point lighting a cigar that was so pungent, I coughed. "Does your father smoke cigars?"

Jenniffer laughed and confirmed, "Tim did like his cigars!"

I replied, "Well, he's havin' one now!"

I did not find out until many weeks after the Reading that Jenniffer had come secretly hoping to talk with her deceased father, and that she was conflicted because he had convinced her to stay in her high-profile job. She wanted to quit but was afraid he would not approve. She was also most anxious to know if he was proud of her, as he hadn't expressed that to her directly while he was alive. She wanted the same thing from her father as she did from her bosses: approval, recognition, and permission to do what her heart told her was best.

While Jenniffer was enamored, as anyone would be, that she was able to feel her father's presence and hear what he had to say, I wanted her to see that her persistent challenge was related to the fear of not being loved because she had not performed well or done enough.

Once she could compassionately understand that her fear of "not enoughness" transcended the circumstances in this life and caused her to give her power to others to judge her, she could make a decision to reclaim her power, voice, and self-trust. When Jenniffer said that she wanted to love and approve of herself without the need to perform, we energetically released the beliefs and patterns that kept her stuck in fear and replaced them with those that enhanced her self-trust.

At the end of the Reading, I still had no idea why the mysterious Jenniffer did not want to reveal her last name. It was only later that I learned she was the inimitable Jenniffer Weigel, Emmy Award–winning broadcast journalist, and that her father, Tim Weigel, had been a sports icon in Chicago for decades.

Jenniffer committed to living more consciously and with conviction. Soon after the Reading, she quit her television journalist job to pursue storytelling with a positive purpose. Although she walked away with more clarity and peace, the Reading didn't mean that her life would be without further struggle regarding her persistent challenge. The difference was that the next time it occurred, she had the knowledge to recognize it and respond differently.

Each time a challenge in this area has arisen since the Reading, such as having only a few people show up to her book launch in a particular city, she struggles, and then remembers to stay true to herself. Jenniffer now believes that no matter what it looks like or feels like in the moment, everything is happening for a reason and for the highest good. This is Jenniffer's new map of reality.

She understands that it takes patience, imagination, and determination to hold onto this belief in the face of evidence that runs counter to it. In fact, what is true for Gandhi or any of us is that only through practiced belief-in-action does inner spirit and personal power grow. As she has persistently strengthened her resolve, she has developed a Collective Force that has positively impacted many others—including me!

Jenniffer's books and her one-woman show, as well as her current Chicago Tribune column and WGN on-air position, give expression to her voice, her power, and her hard-earned self-trust.

From Jenniffer's and other client Readings, I came to understand persistent challenges are creative possibilities for learning about love in the very particular way each of us come to learn it. They are invitations from our soul—the part of us that is always connected to the eternal— to transform the peculiar kind of pain that comes from our deepest fears.

FEAR-BASED BELIEFS, SOUL LESSONS, AND SOURCE LIFETIMES

Fears that swim at the bottom of persistent challenges are primal. They are wrapped in invisible, core beliefs that we are not enough, or that we are unworthy, unwanted, or unlovable. The unconscious mind silently warns us not to explore such stark fears because if they turn out to be true, what then?

In addition, fear of this type, as revealed by Readings, originates in other lives or archetypes and is usually accompanied by shame or guilt…along with companion fears of exposure and humiliation. To prevent humiliation, these fears are covered by qualities most approved of by others—typically essential gifts. From there, the fear wrapped in shame wrapped in essential gifts is delivered back to us in persistent challenges—resulting in the conundrum of not letting ourselves have what we most want.

This can be as simple as having self-judgment because in another life/archetype we failed as a leader because we did not listen to others' opinions or find them of any value. So in this life we are excellent advisors to leaders but can't seem to secure the top position, no matter how qualified we are or how hard we try.

We are stuck here because the qualities we are learning about and which are becoming essential gifts—listening, encouraging, and inspiring others—collide with the desire to lead as well as the hidden fear of bringing our power and leadership to light.

Soul lessons are persistent challenges—what we most yearn for and cannot seem to attain—that contain essential gifts that, in turn, cover core fears. When we make a commitment to befriend inner vulnerability and approach ourselves with compassion, our soul lesson is more likely to unfold and empty its contents. That results in greater freedom to employ the energy formerly invested in a soul lesson on behalf of our heart's desires.

What makes being human so complicated is that while soul lessons are the organizing principles upon which our reality is built, they are hidden from our everyday lives. Therefore, you may say: "Reality has taught me that my fears are true and justified," and that would be accurate.

Soul lessons are tricky because we have to step outside the map of reality that contains and protects them to discover the truth underneath them. As Einstein's wise counsel warns us: "You cannot solve a problem from the same consciousness that created it. You must learn to see the world anew."

RETURNING TO OUTSIDE INFLUENCES: SOURCE LIFETIMES

In Readings, as I witness stories unfold, I have no idea what will happen, much less what themes will emerge. With each new story, the point is foreign to me until it reveals itself. I have found, after many years of observing, that the reason the particular stories I See "light up" is because they represent soul lesson themes in garb that clients can understand, even if it is outside their current experience.

At some point after I began asking Spirit, "Why? Why is it this particular soul lesson for this client?" a response occurred, and I have included it in Readings ever since. It is what I call a "source lifetime." This kind of story represents the very beginning of a particular soul lesson. A source lifetime usually holds the painful memory of a tragedy and conundrum, which results in self-horror and the withholding of self-forgiveness. It then sends us on a path that causes us to learn to love in ways that are limited by self-condemnation and defenses, and yet become essential gifts. Decisions made in this lifetime prevent us from having what we most desire. Here is an example:

My client, Anna, owns a group of day-care centers that have won "best in class" awards. Anna is all business and says she is good at organizing these centers. She leaves the child care "to those whose skills are suited to that task." A few years ago, she met and married a man who wanted several children. Anna put it this way: "I always hoped I could have children and learn to be a good mother; I was just never sure that could happen."

After trying for a long while, a doctor informed Anna that it would be hard for her to become pregnant. They decided to try alternative ways to bear children, and were repeatedly unsuccessful. It had been a long road, and Anna wanted to know if there was anything energetically that was blocking their road to parenthood.

I Saw Anna in several other lives: as a military man helping families during a village invasion; as the strict director of a school for girls, instructing teachers to assure the children were safe; and as a street-wise orphan child who helped other street children to survive.

After the theme of "children and safety" emerged, I could have stopped there and said that she was concerned for children's safety, which is an essential way (gift) that she has become successful in her day-care business. I could have said that in these lifetimes she, herself, felt unsafe and is still unconsciously carrying that feeling. Then I could have recommended she should practice grounding exercises to enhance her feelings of safety.

Instead, another lifetime story appeared. It had a different quality than the others. It felt more intense. I waited and carefully reported the vivid movie that was unfolding before me.

Anna was a nanny who had responsibility for six young children plus her own two. She was competent, thriving, and found joy in her work. One day in the garden, she was helping a few children set up for a game when she heard a scream. Two very young children had found their way through a gap in the fence, and had fallen and landed on a pipe that was camouflaged but not deeply buried. One hit her head and died from the injury, and the other child's injury resulted in a permanently deformed hip. These two were not her children.

Anna was understandably bereft. She was fired for her "irresponsibility." In the face of unspeakable grief, Anna denied her feelings so she could remain strong for her own children as she struggled to survive. At the end of her life, Anna made the decision that she must be hyper-vigilant with children's safety. She also decided she was unworthy to have her own children. She stuffed her pain into her physical tissue, while self-condemnation and punishment replaced honest grief.

Anna was now organizing her life around a fear-based belief that if she was directly responsible for children, they would be in danger. Self-condemnation also assured she would forbid the privilege, station, or circumstance that brought about the tragedy, such as having her own children...and thus a soul lesson was born.

We come into this lifetime and recreate the unfinished business of the other lives, in hopes that we will make a new choice for self-forgiveness and release our self-prohibitions. That is why soul lessons are persistent. Spirit continually asks that we reconsider self-love.

Several months after the Reading, Anna found herself pregnant and has since given birth to a healthy girl. It would not matter from what source her self-forgiveness occurred. Spirit may come to us in the form of an inspiring poster or the kind word of a friend or the story we read in the paper. What matters is that we find the areas in our lives where we have withheld self-love and then free ourselves through forgiveness.

Source lifetimes help us understand the origins of soul lessons. Some clients report that the persistent challenge for which they sought help no longer afflicts them and there are no lingering reminders. In Anna's case, she says she feels complete. However, there may be times when she overprotects her daughter because she is prone to organize around the feeling that children are generally unsafe. Now she can notice when she does that and understand it. Just as in Jenniffer's case, Anna can have an ongoing relationship with her new self, recognizing that when the old self appears, she can apply compassionate understanding.

LIFE PURPOSE

A vast majority of clients want to know the nature of their life's purpose. Often they are referring to the best career fit. While work can be a wonderful expression of creativity and meaning, life purpose may have little to do with a job or work. I have certainly never Seen, for example, a call for someone to become a vice president of a particular insurance company.

We all share a human journey on this planet, and we have the same elements that define life purpose.

The first element is to identify, develop, enjoy and share our essential gifts. We are each unique in the universe. Even if we can identify other lifetimes, this one, now, is a first and only. What do we love? What brings us energy? What aspect of what we are doing lifts our spirits? If we do not contemplate or attempt to express this, we lose the opportunity to fulfill this element of our life's purpose.

The second element is to gain the unique wisdom we came to learn by identifying and releasing the fear and fear-based beliefs that limit our light and joy. The invisible, subtle, insidious, embedded fears that get in our way and keep us from our heart's desire are waiting in the dark to reveal the wisdom with which they are encoded.

They are soul lessons that will remain with us for as long as it takes us to find them. The intention to unearth hidden wisdom, the courage to face the fears that cover our soul lessons, and the persistent practice with whatever methodology feels helpful and appropriate will fulfill the second element of our life's purpose.

The third element is to rediscover and realize the Oneness to which we belong. This is only possible when heartfelt forgiveness, compassion, mercy and kindness are the central tools of our relationship with ourselves and others. Without these, judgment rules, and exclusion is seen as an intelligent strategy for sorting good from bad...and through free will, leaves us unentitled to our birthright of the experience of Oneness.

The nature of our journey is to discover that humanity itself is a costume rendered so we can gain perspective about the particular way we deny love, and the many ways we can engage and expand love's influence.

We are ultimately here to remember and act out of our wholeness. We must intersect with soul lessons if we are to align with our life

226

purpose. Purpose is not only about the contribution we make in our lifetimes—it is about the quality of our relationship with ourselves, which then forms the quality of the contribution we make. It's less what we do and more how we do it that makes the difference to our souls and the souls of fellow students/teachers on the path.

DESTINY POINTS

When clients ask me about whether they have a destiny regarding a particular relationship, I find myself back in my uncomfortable seat with Judy Tergis, the psychic teacher in San Francisco. It was there I learned more about free will and the choices I could make regarding the energies and entities that persistently knocked at my door.

It made me wonder about the nature of free will and the characters in life that I attract, as well as situations in which I feel without control—and especially when it comes to particular relationships that I would swear up and down are entirely unrelated to my free will.

I discovered a response to these deliberations over time, as I began to Read "destiny points" on clients' energy fields. These show up as a firm stake in the ground on someone's invisible map and indicate that they are immutable. Apparently, there are people whom we have signed up to encounter in this life prior to our birth, though our free will dictates in what role or capacity they impact us.

There are destiny points where we find ourselves intimately involved in a situation beyond our control, though our free will dictates how we respond. There are specific lessons we came to learn, and our free will dictates how faithfully we learn them as our minds and egos deeply influence the shape of our learning.

One client, Marty, was happily married. She went on a business trip to Europe and there met a man who was so compelling that she was embarrassed. Marty would not cheat on her husband, but she said she could not stop thinking of this man. "How can a complete stranger feel so intimate and familiar? We just clicked right away like we'd known each other forever." She didn't understand the attraction and wanted it to stop.

When I looked at her name and his name together, I Saw a movie in which they were best childhood friends, with Jay being the risk taker who was prompting Marty to "go for it." It was only when Marty was with Jay that she felt brave enough to move out of herself, and then feel happy and proud of herself.

"You are entering a season of life," I said, "where your soul is prompting you to move out of your comfort zone and to go beyond what has been familiar. It's time to reclaim your power in this way. Meeting Jay reminded you that it is possible to do what is uncomfortable and then to enjoy it."

Marty inhaled. "I was just asked to take on a promotion—a liaison role at work that would require me to have to work with leaders who intimidate me. I was thinking of saying no." She thought for a moment.

"This makes perfect sense!" she said finally. "When I was with Jay in Europe, I felt like I could fly. Now that I know I can fly, I don't need Jay's company to feel that way!"

Marty later reported that she took the promotion and that she was no longer "obsessed" with thoughts of Jay. "But when I feel small inside, I think of Jay and it gives me courage."

Destiny points stimulate spiritual DNA to awaken us to an impending transformational season of life. While they have a place on the invisible map of reality, free will plays a major role in defining how we respond to and relate to moments of destiny.

ALWAYS LEARNING LOVE

As the contents on the invisible map of reality became clearer—essential gifts, fear-based beliefs, persistent challenges/soul lessons, life purpose, and destiny points—I learned one final piece of significant content from Readings that reminded me that life is one whole story, and it is only about love.

I began to See that whatever limitation we impose from a lifetime where fear became the organizing principle, we continue to love around it. Like a tree that integrates a fence into its trunk as it evolves, our growth does not abate. Shaping the path of our love through fear-based beliefs, we may become, like Marianne, scrupulously good at sensing others' needs, or like Anna, exquisitely attentive to the safety needs of children and to protecting innocence. Remember that the fear itself is born of the shame that says, "I wish I had loved differently so this would not have occurred."

The end game is to ask for and receive forgiveness, and to forgive others, and then reclaim the gift left behind. In the instance of the leader who refused to take the top position but instead became an advisor, when she reclaims her leadership, she brings greater humility with it. In reclaiming her wholeness, she can be a better leader.

It is true that shame can cause someone to become embittered and either strike out at those around him or turn anger inward and destroy himself. In these cases, he is expressing the self-hatred he feels and is projecting it or trying to protect others from knowing him—as he feels unworthy of love. If you find yourself in a relationship with a person like this, beyond taking steps to remove yourself if you decide that is best, continue to send love from the God of your heart into the heart of the self-hating person. And ask for the love you send to knock at his door in moments when he is undefended.

If he is open, it will help heal him. If he is not, your blessing will return to you. Or, if you are honestly working your way through a difficult time, dedicate your work to the one person you most do not want to love. That heals parts of your invisible map of reality that are related to this person's presence in your life, and reminds you of the power you hold in your free will to love.

Life is, indeed, one whole story.

REFLECTION

The invisible map of reality repositions persistent challenges so we recognize them as our soul knocking at the door, begging us to reconsider the fearful foundations upon which these challenges are based. Appreciating the essential gifts that cover our deepest fear, and committing to self-compassion, give us the qualities we need to do our human homework in the service of our life's purpose. Destiny points tell us when it is imperative to address fears or say hello to our expanding selves.

While stories of other lifetimes may offer rich context from which to understand soul lessons, they are but one way, one method, for allowing the self-compassion and courage necessary to release whatever keeps us from love.

Part III: *Intuition as an Intelligence*

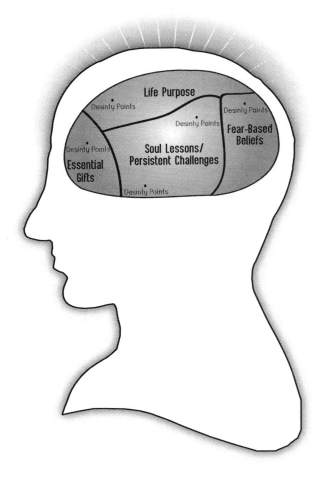

Now that the invisible map of reality has been made visible, this question remains: How can it be regularly accessed and engaged?

Part III advocates for intuition to be the bridge between painfully persistent challenges and the truth and wisdom encoded in our invisible map of reality so that we can realign on our path. Intuition is explored here not as an occasional "hit" but as an intelligence that is meant to be developed.

Reinforcing this position as critically important is the phenomenon of an increasing number of children born with high intuitive giftedness, who are regularly being misdiagnosed as "learning disordered." The following examples of intuitive Readings with children reveal the possibility of supporting a more informed and developmental path of coping for these children rather than the most common coping method, a medicated path. Once a new map of reality is embraced, these children can forward solutions to challenges for which logic and reason are insufficient or not sufficiently swift enough to assure a sustainable future.

CHAPTER TWELVE

Misdiagnosing Gifted Children

At one point, as I moved into my early forties, I was traveling around the world working as a business consultant while intuitively Reading clients in my Chicago office when I was at home. I had begun to think about adoption. I decided to visit friends who had children to remind myself of what it meant to make that choice. On one of those weekend visits, I stayed with a childhood friend of mine, Nancy, who had a son, Sam.

Nancy and I were part of the same social group in high school. Since I rarely talked about my spiritual experiences and Nancy had moved out of town, she was not aware of them. She knew me as a person who was religious because I went to Mass all the time, but as an adult, she related to the side of me that worked in the business world.

Several years before, I visited Nancy when Sam was an infant and noticed that he would not focus on me when I interacted with him. Sam looked up at the ceiling a lot, as if there were some fascinating things going on up there. He was easily distracted—not really paying attention to the immediate goings on, and seemingly off in his own world. This boy was definitely "different." Even before his first birthday, I could see he did not respond quickly or with the kind of alertness that other children expressed.

As a young boy, Sam began to exhibit a variety of quirky gifts. For example, he would listen to a video or story for the first time and be able to recite it verbatim. He had a vivid imagination and could make up plays about anything. It was like he had a whole theater group in his head.

Yet his abilities in math and in other basic grade-school subjects were below average, and his grades continually trailed behind his classmates. He was highly disorganized and could not remember many simple facts, nor could he understand the nature of his homework assignments, even when his teacher took special time out to explain them to him.

I did not have the opportunity to visit Sam often when he was young, though he knew me as "Aunt Therese." On this visit, I walked into the kitchen and saw Sam moving his body in ways that I would refer to as "moving to the energy running through him," as mine had at times after Mass when I was a child.

I could Feel his energy was scattered. I had an immediate urge to move my hands and quiet his vibration. I called him to me and began asking him questions about baseball. Quite unconsciously, my hands began to make gentle sweeping movements around him as I talked. Surprisingly, Sam suddenly stood stock-still, the way children do when you softly caress their heads when they are tired.

There are many times when working in business or with an individual that my hands begin to move in ways my conscious mind cannot decipher. Until recent years, there was a lag time between what I was doing and what occurred to me about its rationale. In this case, it took me a few moments to realize that Sam was out of his body, and my hands were facilitating the grounding he needed to bring him back into his physical self.

My hands swept over him and made very particular gestures at different points over several minutes. I remember thinking, "I hope Nancy doesn't walk in right now. I'd have a really hard time explaining this."

As if on cue, she appeared at the door, looking bewildered as she witnessed the situation.

"Busted," I thought. "Now what am I going to say?!" As is often the case, my hands would not stop until this informal "session" was over. Nancy continued to watch as my mind raced, trying to think of a way to explain.

When it was finally complete, my hands stopped, and I said something to Sam about his favorite baseball player. At that moment, Nancy could see that not only was her normally jittery son uncharacteristically calm, but then he turned around, threw his arms around my legs, and said, "Thank you, Aunt Therese."

I blushed as I said, "You're welcome, Sam!" and he ran out of the room like he was headed for an ice-cream truck.

When his mother finally asked what was going on, I stalled, searching for words that would make sense to a "non–energy-oriented" person. I could think of nothing clever, so I blurted out, "Well, Sam is vibrating at a frequency faster than his physical body can accommodate, so I was slowing down his frequency and grounding him."

I rolled my eyes at myself, thinking that was probably the least helpful way I could have expressed it. I expected Nancy to escort me to the front door to protect her child from my eccentricities.

Instead she replied, "No, I mean what were you doing with your hands?"

I was shocked by her question and tried to understand why she might be asking. I explained to her that the movement of my hands was how grounding energy came through me for others.

"Oh," Nancy replied. And then she just stared at me for a long moment. I wondered if she had somehow experienced this herself. Instead, much to my surprise, she said, "When Sam was a toddler, he used to move his hands just like that—the way your hands were moving around him."

I knew at that moment that Sam had intuitive gifts like mine. Despite this revelation, and as is true for many other children, Sam was later diagnosed as learning disordered—specifically ADHD—and put on daily medication for more than a decade. I completely understood that when medicated, Sam felt better about himself at school and was more successful in his traditional public school's expectations.

Nancy and her husband remain loving, caring parents who attended to Sam's needs and helped every way they knew how. Sam is now in college, exploring his many exceptional gifts in theater and the arts. He is afraid to get off the medication, as he says his energy feels jittery and disjointed when he attempts it.

I'm grateful for Sam's success and that his parents love him dearly. However, I also know the medication prevents Sam from accessing, exploring, and developing his energetic/spiritual gifts, and that he may never know that potential. Certainly he has no map of reality to date that would offer him that possibility.

That is when I began to wonder what it would be like if everyone understood intuition as an intelligence. What would it be like if everyone had to learn about their intuition as a part of their life's purpose? What would happen if everyone knew how to manage their energy and direct it in the service of others?

Instead of stumbling into different healing modalities such as Reiki and Healing Touch as adults, what if all schools included the exploration of questions such as these: How are you intuitive? In what way do you most often access wisdom? Do you Hear words, See pictures, Feel or Sense things, or Know from your heart?

What if everyone understood their intuitive preference just as clearly as they knew their preference as an introvert or extrovert? Would "learning disorders" become a thing of the past? My head was spinning. My visit with Nancy made me wonder if I could make a contribution to changing the way people perceive children who are spiritually and intuitively gifted and who are labeled as learning disordered.

Around this time, I learned that my fiancé, Paul, had changed his mind about having children, but still wanted to marry. Based on my emerging interest in and passion for children, as well as on my intuition that told me I would have a child in this lifetime, we gently parted ways, remaining close friends.

MISUNDERSTANDING GIFTED CHILDREN

Within a year after my visit with Nancy, I received a call from journalist Jenniffer Weigel, whose Reading I referred to earlier. Well after the

Reading, Jen wrote *Stay Tuned* and *I'm Spiritual, Dammit!*, two books that generously provided greater public exposure to my intuitive Readings.

On this day, Jen said she'd had a recent phone session with a psychic in New York who told her that she was working with a woman named "Therese." When Jen gave her a neutral "uh-huh" response, the woman began to recite a past life wherein Jen was the renowned investigative journalist Nelly Bly, and I was a physician in an insane asylum.

I was against drugs and chains, which apparently were quite popular at the time, and tried to take the patients off their medications and get them to move. I said that if patients were walked around in the sunlight, they would get better. Nelly/Jen went undercover as a patient and ended up reporting about my unconventional methods. Her article allowed the method to become more accepted, and other institutions began to follow suit.

The most fascinating part of this tale for me was when Jen called me and recounted it over the phone. The minute she said, "You were an insane asylum doc," I doubled over and began to sob. My reaction was severe and immediate. Suddenly, I could see people all around me who were misunderstood and drugged because those in charge knew no other answer. I struggled to listen to the rest of the story, putting the phone on mute so Jen would not hear my unstoppable sobs.

I had no idea the parallels that would begin to emerge after Jen asked me to accompany her the following week to a meeting whose topic was gifted children. I had a last-minute appointment cancellation and decided to accept. Due to a wild set of circumstances that followed, I later found myself on a flight to Utah to attend a conference on gifted children. As I began to talk with medical and academic experts in this field, I was shocked to learn that those I interviewed unanimously agreed that dangerous drugs were being dispensed with very little expert analysis, and that as a result, we, as a nation, are losing our best and brightest children.

Jen and I decided to partner to coproduce a DVD called *The Misdiagnosis of Gifted Children*, after a book by the same name. The DVD contains the opinions of medical doctors specializing in children with learning disorders, pediatric neuropsychologists, the president of the National Association for Gifted Children, professors who work with profoundly gifted children, and parents of children diagnosed as learning disordered—some called "twice exceptional."[2]

Several of the experts interviewed were coauthors with Jim Webb, PhD, in their book *The Misdiagnosis of Gifted Children and Adults.* Dr. Webb is founder of an organization called Supporting the Emotional Needs of Gifted Children, which funded the DVD, and Dr. Webb's organization works closely with The National Association of Gifted Children.

When I did additional background research for the DVD, I became more alarmed. The Center for Disease Control documented staggering statistics on the number of children receiving what the US government labels "class III drugs," whose chemical makeup is as close to methamphetamine (commonly known as "crystal meth") as can be found.

---

[2] 2 National Association of Gifted Children, *The Misdiagnosis of Gifted Children DVD*, 2006, a JCW production.

As of December 2011, the CDC reported that 9.5 percent or 5.4 million children in the US ages four to seventeen were diagnosed with ADD and ADHD, and more that 66 percent of those were given class III prescription drugs.[3]

These drugs have not been proven safe for children, and no longitudinal studies have been conducted to document potential long-term impacts or side effects. My body reacted as strongly to these facts as it did when Jen recalled my life as an insane-asylum physician. I painfully flashed on the millions of misunderstood children. I wondered how many of them were, as one pediatric neuropsychologist interviewed in the DVD put it, "nearly dysfunctional even to basic tasks because of the medications and their side effects."

After all I read on this topic I found a quote from Albert Einstein which summed up my feelings:

"The intuitive mind is a sacred gift and the rational mind is a faithful servant. We have created a society that honors the servant and has forgotten the gift."

Dr. Webb's book and the DVD have helped many parents and school administrators assure that they do not make the mistake of recommending a diagnosis such as ADD or ADHD for any child without a full assessment by a pediatric neuropsychologist. Yet I felt the rising epidemic of labeling children with learning disorders, and then providing drugs so that they could meet the standards of a traditional

---

[3] Centers for Disease Control and Prevention, ADHD, Data and Statistics, "Increasing Prevalence of Parent-Reported Attention-Deficit/Hyperactivity Disorder Among Children—United States, 2003 and 2007," (November 12, 2010) 59(44): 1439–1443.

school system, to be very suspect.

The medical experts I interviewed from across the country were convinced that a good percentage of these kids are acting out because they are academically gifted and unchallenged. In fact, the president of the National Association of Gifted Children estimated through their studies that about 80 percent of school violence is perpetrated by gifted and talented children whose anger at being overlooked and underserved is expressed in powerfully negative ways.

Other children are called "twice exceptional" because they have a high IQ and also express symptoms similar to ADD and ADHD behaviors. However, these symptoms are a result of their giftedness, not a general pathology. I was dizzy with these facts, studies and stories.

It should not take an experienced systems consultant to ask this question: "When does a rising epidemic become a question of an inadequate system rather than a problem with the kids who are being labeled and taught by that system?" I read books by medical doctors who were in agreement that the system, rather than the children, was at cause for this phenomenon.

One author and professor, Sir Ken Robinson, offered an informative perspective in his presentation "Changing Education Paradigms," which can now be found on YouTube. He showed some statistics on ADD and ADHD and the associated drugs, a treatment that he said "anesthetizes" rather than "wakes up" children at a time when we most need their creative engagement. He claims that learning-disorder diagnoses are a fad, similar to doctors taking patients' tonsils out whenever a sore throat was diagnosed in the 1960s and 1970s.

Even after researching statistics and reading theories about the phenomenon of "learning disorders," I remained in deep compassion for the nearly impossible challenges that must be navigated by parents who have children who exhibit behaviors very different from their peers.

I have heard about how the diagnosis and drugs have enabled some children to retrieve their self-esteem, find friends, and do well in school. I have seen how families have felt healed by one child being able to do better in school because of the extra help he is provided by law as a result of a "disorder" diagnosis.

My concern for the children and their future is not laced with judgment about what parents determine is best for their child. There are few alternatives that are financially viable for most parents.

Having said that, after producing the DVD, I wanted to know more about what else I could contribute to perspectives that forward a healthy, positive, and more supportive future for our children and their development. In particular, I thought about how many of children labeled with disorders were diagnosed because they exhibited the same symptoms as me, or as Sam, with hands moving in ways that I now understand as healing but may easily be misinterpreted.

BUT NOT THOSE GIFTS

When I inquired as to medical and academic experts' awareness of intuitively and spiritually gifted children, I watched the extreme discomfort in their body language. They truly wanted to distance the label "gifted" from those children.

One professor emeritus I interviewed, who taught profoundly gifted children and teens in special schools, admitted toward the end of the interview that she was a closet intuitive—and was frank about saying she could not reveal that part of her giftedness to her colleagues or she would not be considered credible. So even among the children who are marginalized because of their academic giftedness, intuitively gifted children are outside their margins!

Thinking about how we come to understand ourselves in the first place, I realized that as children, we receive and process stimuli in our own unique way. We do not have constructs for making meaning of "our way" until someone differentiates it and instructs us—through role modeling or teaching. Parents cannot change their children's uniqueness, but they do help children make sense and meaning of their gifts and experiences, whether or not parents are aware of this important role.

If parents' map of reality is not big enough, or if parents do not have the same kind of experiences as their child, it is a normal reaction to feel fear on behalf of the child. Anything outside the parent's box of "normality" may be construed as "disordered" and also unsafe, because it is outside the order that parents use to make sense of their world.

On the other hand, much of the quality of our life experience is determined by what questions we ask. When we frame a question in these terms: "What is wrong with my child?" we have already allowed for the coloring of others' judgments and perspectives. If instead we asked, "How is my child gifted?" the lens we are using would have a much wider angle, and open up the possibility of different kinds of support.

PSYCHIC CHILDREN

Hoping to find out more specifically about the world of spiritually and intuitively gifted children, I attended a conference hosted by James Twyman, for and about psychic children. Loading my digital video camera into my suitcase, I headed to Ashland, Oregon.

I was duly impressed with the children I interviewed. Some reported how they could See into a person's body and what part needed healing; some could put their hands near a person's body, and the person would report that he felt better. Others said they felt called to be spiritual counselors and recited the miracles that their prayer partner had experienced after they prayed with her. I was perhaps even more impressed with what happened when my camera was not rolling.

Walking to the parking lot to find my car, I noticed a group of about eight children ranging in age from about six to twelve. As I walked by, not one of them looked up, but I was taken aback by what they were doing. Each held a spoon in his or her hand. They were teasing and chiding each other in competition.

"Ah, you are so slow. Watch this!" said one boy. He then stared at the spoon in his hand, and it bent backward as if it were a clock in a Salvador Dali painting.

I was dumbfounded, feeling as though I were an extra in the movie *The Matrix*. I watched as each of them—some effortlessly, some with clear concentration—bent the spoon using only the power of their mind.

Back inside the conference, I talked with another participant, Mike, who was the principal of a residential boys school in Canada. He said that when kids were misbehaving, teachers would send them to his office. Rather than punishing them for bad behavior, Mike's method was to gain the trust of each student to find out what was really going on under the misbehavior. What he discovered, he said, changed his life.

One boy, for example, after hesitating a long time, admitted that he was distracted because he was worried about a teacher.

"Why are you worried about Ms. Stechell?" Mike asked.

"Well...I See colors around people," the boy said. "And Ms. S. has the color brown around her lungs. I think she might be ill." It was that same teacher who sent the boy to the office because "he was not paying attention."

After Mike worked out a way to tell the teacher, she went to the doctor, and they found a spot on her lung. Successful treatment followed.

"We keep telling these kids, 'You're not paying attention,'" Mike expressed with frustration, "when, in fact, they are paying far more attention than we have the capability to do!"

Another time, Mike said, there was a kid who said he was distracted by what was going on in China. "What do you mean?" asked a bewildered Mike.

Then Mike stopped his story and said to me, "There are no televisions, newspapers, videos, or cell phones allowed in the school, so I knew he could not have gotten any information about China from those sources."

The boy then described the rioting he'd "Seen" while "the teacher blathered on about fractions." When Mike prompted the boy to be more explicit, he described the scene in such vivid detail that it was as if he were one of the particular people involved exactly where the riots were taking place. Mike found a news source and was dumbfounded by the fact that the boy had recited details that were late-breaking news several hours after his meeting with him. In other words, the boy would have had to be there to know what he knew.

Mike said he'd researched and found a phenomenon called "bi-locating," where a person can be present in two places at once. As he described this, I remembered reading *Cosmic Voyage* by Courtney Brown, PhD, an associate professor of economics. Dr. Brown wrote about how he was trained by the US army to bi-locate so he could assist in spying on Russian satellites. Mike said that kids with these abilities scare us, so the kids and their gifts go unrecognized and unacknowledged. He agreed with Dr. Jim Webb, whose book he had read, that we are losing our best and brightest through misunderstanding or misinterpreting their behavior—only he was talking about intuitively gifted children rather than academically gifted ones.

In addition to the feats I captured on tape and through simple observation, I was educated by the adults' attitudes regarding their children. In one of the networking groups, I sat next to a woman named Elizabeth, who was professionally dressed and whose speech and manner were quietly elegant and respectful.

Each person was asked to explain what brought him or her to the conference. When it was her turn, Elizabeth said very firmly and calmly,

"I have the extraordinary privilege of being the single parent of a child who is deaf and labeled 'autistic.' When people meet my son, Todd, they often make their observations known as to how normal he really is. They seem insistent on saying things to assure me that he appears to be pretty much like other children. But my son did not come to this planet to be normal. My son came to teach us something…he came to teach us something…and no one is listening."

I was struck by how Elizabeth related to the word "normal." That her son should "fit in" was irrelevant to her. In fact, it seemed to me that if Todd were entirely "normal," relative to a select group of his peers, his mother would still find this information irrelevant and continue to ask the same question: "What did my son come to teach us?"

Elizabeth has encountered deeply painful challenges in raising and supporting Todd.

Despite this, she chooses to perceive him differently. She is listening in to try to understand who her son is and how to honor him—his presence, his gifts, and his purpose.

This extraordinary woman made a deep impression on me. I kept her words in my heart: "How can we listen to our children so that we can begin to understand who they are in spirit and what they came to teach us?" Little did I know that I was about to find out—in a way that was very close to home.

REFLECTION

Early experiences of my intuitive and spiritual gifts have enhanced my compassion for and understanding of the millions of children who are daily misunderstood and misdiagnosed—by those who have not known such experience or found its positive potential.

How can we create a new map of reality that includes intuitive giftedness so these children can be seen, heard and given pathways for the development of their gifts?

CHAPTER THIRTEEN

One Light Leaves and Another Arrives

As the intensity of this journey in uncovering intuitive children continued, I was faced with some intimate personal experiences that marked the unexpected beginning of my entry into Reading children and gathering greater insight to inform my now academically piqued imagination. It started with a very sad event wherein I learned about the relationship between loss and safety.

I found that when we lose what has been closest to our sense of safety and most natural to the way we define ourselves, all maps of reality can stop working. That is precisely what happened for me when my father said a long good-bye through his journey with cancer. My father was kind and gentle. He was wise and sensitive. He was my rock. I had no idea that my sense of safety and whatever grounding I felt in this world was due in large part to his presence...until he left. Despite my ability to "call in those who have passed," I was as helpless as when the Dark Night first threw its shadow upon my path.

Using spiritual and intuitive skills requires a kind of neutrality that cannot be found when, despite reaching the age of forty plus, one only wants "my daddy back." Whatever abilities I had amassed through faithfully groping in the dark for years, they were once again put on hold. I was blind as a bat.

A HAND ACROSS THE MILES

It was perhaps this condition, as well as the desire to replace the warm, fatherly blanket that surrounded me for a lifetime, that prompted me to meet, date, and marry a good man within months following my father's passing. Perhaps life waits for these moments to bring us people and lessons that we otherwise would not allow because we are "too smart to let that happen." I did Know from flashes, dreams, and experience that the relationship would take me through shadow lands where I did not want to go—and from which I would learn in the same painfully awkward way I did during the Dark Night. I did not know I could stumble so far down the rabbit hole. Coming out the other side a few years later, I was wiser—though not unscathed.

It started, however, with that sense that a kind blanket was close by. Even before we married, Tom generously said he wanted to support my dream of adoption, and so we began the paperwork. When we finally received her photograph and information, it just so happened that she was an Aries, just like me. On the Chinese astrological chart, wherein each animal shows up every twelve years, Ana is a monkey, just like me. Tom and I had been married at Catalyst Ranch, a place that was all about creativity and play. We set a sacred space for the ceremony, but somehow the staff had failed to notice that a smiling, stuffed monkey was wrapped around the base of a light near where we said our vows. It showed up in the wedding photos.

Once in China, Tom took one look at Fu Pei Yun and knew he was there not only to support my dream but to also fulfill a dream he did not know he had until that moment. At the ripe age of forty-six, we adopted our daughter, whose name we changed to Ana Joy Pei.

Having spent quite a bit of my childhood observing my wise mother and helping out with my eight younger siblings, I felt capable and ready to fulfill this dream of child rearing. Then reality said a rigorous hello, and sleepless days and nights followed, dragging on for months.

Many times I wondered how my mother, who ably raised eleven of us before the invention of Pampers or permanent-press everything, ever got out of bed in the morning. The physical and mental work of organizing and remembering details of diapers, wipes, snacks, extra clothes, and bottles, while assuring Ana didn't hurt herself as she began running the minute she knew her legs could walk, took up a lot more mindshare than I anticipated.

Her social, psychological, and spiritual development, which I loftily imagined I would be calmly transmitting on a daily basis, was not even on my radar screen. Survival was my first priority, which translated into getting through the day without saying no so often, or raising my voice in panic or worry, as Ana found the street as happy a place to greet with glee as the sidewalk next to me.

Having lived through the first few years, riding that parent-only roller coaster between highs of unspeakable joy and gratitude and lows of horrific shame and guilt for my ignorance and reactions to some of Ana's emotional needs, I sometimes found time to move beyond survival. With each year that Ana's independence grew, my angst slowly subsided. I discovered that high stress decreases even the loudest inner voices that try to offer guidance. Rather than learn from the wisdom within, I would have to learn from my mistakes.

One night, a few days before I was to go out of town on business for the first time, I told my then five-year-old daughter about it. When she began to whimper, I felt both guilty and scared of her reactions. I immediately said, "Let's not focus on it now. I won't be going for a few days. Let's do something fun." She seemed to quickly change moods, and I felt relieved.

The next morning, Ana seemed a bit crankier than usual and did not want to comply with my continual requests to perform the usual morning routine before school. She wanted my help with everything she had been doing on her own for a while. "I need help with my shoes" (they were Velcroix); "help me wash my face," "brush my hair," "no, that's not how I want it," and on and on it went.

I became frustrated because I had a meeting for which I also had preparation to do. After a time-out and more "acting out," I finally sat next to her and stopped talking. I felt angry but also helpless. I could feel that whatever I was saying or doing was not working. I said a prayer to ask how I might best address the situation.

Suddenly, Spirit seemed to emerge from within me. I looked deeply into her eyes and said, "I'll miss you too, baby." Then we both burst into big crocodile tears and hugged each other until we were finished.

With all the agendas of parenthood, it is often difficult to make room for children's feelings, much less our own. I've found guilt to be an unhappy and constant companion in the journey of parenting. Its companionship often motivates me to bypass or delay dealing with difficult feelings in the moment. Ultimately, these feelings grow in the dark, hidden behind other events. With time, they become displaced and come out in more painful ways.

I was afraid of making mistakes that would emotionally and permanently scar my child. This was accompanied by my parental instinct to protect my child from pain along with the belief that it was my job to minimize my daughter's discomfort if at all possible.

Eventually I began to understand that minimizing Ana Joy's pain as an organizing principle shortchanges her learning about how to allow and befriend her feelings. I thought about the discipline of holding back my feelings or the act of distracting Ana from hers.

I was accustomed to thinking of discipline as the act of staying in control of myself. I then realized that discipline can also be thought of as the act of telling the part of me that wants to express something to be quiet. It is often an "against" energy. When properly embraced as a positive value, discipline allows us to become mature in our responses to others and to our work or practice.

When used as a weapon to silence what we find unacceptable, it is ineffective and sends the message to the body to stuff those feelings into physical tissue or into the unconscious, where they will later be displaced. As parents, it is easy to use our power to get our way, especially at the moment we are angrily telling our children that they cannot always get theirs. I've also found myself raising my voice, while telling Ana not to raise hers.

While phrases like "emotional intelligence" sound very important and lofty, they come down to some very simple principles on the invisible map of reality. Beliefs are accompanied by feelings, whether happy, sad, angry, or fearful. According to the literature and what I have observed in my work, anger covers sadness that covers fear. Therefore, anger is typically unspoken sadness covering a fear that is likely related to shame or guilt.

Empathy, the ability to first patiently address the feelings of the communicator rather than react or move to fix a perceived problem, is one of the most needed and least modeled skills of our time. It is an essential skill for parenthood.

There are many roles a parent is asked to play in a child's life. Part of our role as parents—perhaps the one I have learned is most important—includes a kind of neutrality. Through that neutrality, we can be aware that a child is not as a reputation gainer or loser, nor is she failure or success for me, as the parent. Rather she is an independent spirit who is evolving in her own time and way. When we hold this view of our children, we can move with greater ease to a place of curiosity and compassion—not assuming we understand what fuels their expression.

PAPA RETURNS

One day when Ana just turned three years old, she was taking a nap on my bed while I was meditating. When she woke up, she rubbed her eyes and sleepily said, "Mama, you Papa is hew."

"My dad is here?" I echoed, knowing she had never physically met my father, who passed over one year before Ana arrived.

"Yeth, he's wite over dare," she said as she pointed to the armoire across from the bed.

"What is he doing?" I asked, amazed that with all my intuitive experience I could not perceive what seemed so clear to her.

"He's smiling," she said. "And he's wit his fwends," she added.

"Who else is there?" I asked.

"Dare's him and him and him and him," she said, pointing as though there were a line of people.

"What are their names?" I asked.

"Emma and Emma and Emma and Emma," she replied, saying the name she applied to everyone and everything. "But dat's just what I call dem. Dey are you fwends."

There it was. My three-year-old could See my father—the very man I could not reach with my medium capacities.

"Of course," I thought. "How could it be any other way?"

Ana is an old soul and a wise one. I learn by listening to what she notices and says. Sometimes she stares at me with a very neutral look when I have said something in anger that I realize later is altogether about me and not about her. I have no doubt about who, in this relationship, is teaching whom.

READING INTUITIVE CHILDREN

In addition to Seeing my deceased father, Ana was showing other signs of her intuitive gifts. Her dad, who lived next door after our divorce, consistently reported of this four-year-old, "Ana says everything I'm thinking. Sometimes I think about something specific just to test her, and she says it exactly as I'm thinking about it!"

At the same time as Ana was demonstrating her gifts, intuitive

Reading clients who were parents began to ask me to Read their children so they could better understand them—especially the parents who, after a moment of thinking about how to describe their children, called them "quirky."

Once in my office, parents would share "unusual" stories about their children with me in hushed tones, as if they were afraid that someone outside the door might hear and judge their child as having or being "a problem." Many of these children had been diagnosed as "learning disordered," and the parents were struggling with the diagnosis or recommended treatment. I intimately felt these parents' struggle to understand their children's behavior—behavior that was off the map of their own reality.

One mother told me about her daughter, Jade, for example, who could See colors around people. Jade told her mother how the colors would get brighter when people were happier and darker when they were unhappy or afraid. Jade also noted how, when the math teacher started his lessons, the color around the girls would suddenly go dark all at once.

Another mother, Sharon, told me her daughter reported that she had been Sharon's father in her last life and then accurately described her father's last few days in the hospital before he passed over—well before her daughter was born.

Some children were fixated on one topic to the exclusion of others, so that they did not socially fit in. Others were brilliant and yet had a hard time in school. Some talked to angels and others Saw orbs (small balls of light).

So, in addition to my ongoing work with professionals and leaders who often became both business-consulting clients and intuitive Reading clients, I began to Read their children.

"LET THE LITTLE CHILDREN COME TO ME"

To intuitively Read a child or teen, I asked that the parent phone in or come into my office and say the child's full name. With that, I look at different aspects of the child's energy field, depending upon the challenge the parent brought to the table: the child's essential gifts that appear through symbols or other lives; the way the child is "energetically wired" around fears; the best choices for schools, teachers, or situations; or the relationships between parent and child.

Readings have revealed that each parent chooses his or her child and the child chooses the parent, for reasons that may make no sense in present time, especially given the pain children can evoke or the intense gifts they bring.

Since this road began, young people have begun to ask their parents if they can see me in my office. I have directly talked with kids as young as seven and up through the teen years. I have been surprised at their willingness and proactive desire to talk with a stranger about energy. I decided to run a six-week Jedi Camp for tweens and teens to see what I could learn and share. My experiences with them have added a whole dimension to the invisible map of reality.

The kids want a clearer explanation of why they perceive as they do; the meaning of their perceptions; what, if anything, they should do about what they perceive; and if possible, how to manage and control the energy they feel or the perceptions that may come unbidden. Like me, they want to know if they have choices, what they are, and what to do with and about their sensitivities.

IT'S ALL IN THE NUMBERS

Seven-year-old Elle could See and talk with spirits she Saw at home. She also Saw numbers over people's heads related to their goodness. The lower the number, the better the person. Going to lunch with her and her father, who is also a closet intuitive, we asked Elle to tell us the number she Saw over the head of our surly waitress.

Elle declared unequivocally, "Thirty-four."

"Elle," I asked gently, "do you know that you have a very big heart? Do you know that your heart is a gift?"

She nodded quietly, her big eyes open wide behind her thick glasses.

"I know it, too, Elle. I can see your big heart. And you know what? You have this gift of Seeing numbers over people's head so you can help them."

Elle nodded slowly, with a little less certitude this time.

"So here's what we're going to do," I said conspiratorially. "You look at me and I'll look at you. But we will send love and light through our hearts to the waitress over there." I pointed to the counter at which our waitress was bent over, calculating bills. "Just keep looking at me, Elle. And we'll see if we can lower her number."

Elle smiled all the way to her ears.

After only fifteen seconds or so, the waitress turned around and looked at our table, and then turned back to her duties. Another ten seconds and the waitress turned around again, while Elle and I continued to stare at each other. Finally, as though she couldn't stand it anymore, after another ten seconds, the waitress stood over us and said nicely, but with some confusion in her voice, "Is there anything I can get you or do for you?"

Elle and I shook our heads as we continued staring at each other with slight smiles on our faces now, while Elle's dad said happily, "No, thanks!"

"Well, Elle, what is her number now?" I asked after the waitress left.

"Thirty-one" she replied.

"Do you see, Elle? It was less than a minute that we sent her love, and already her number is going down. You have a gift to know where someone is at any moment and a gift to send them love to help them feel even closer to Spirit. Do you get it?"

Elle grinned and nodded.

No matter how far off our map of reality our children's quirky ways or talents are, we can find a way to help them see they have a gift, appreciate their power with that gift, and create ways to help them use those gifts to make a positive difference.

"I'M A DEPRESSED AND ANXIOUS TEEN"

Some children want to know how and why they know things, and others feel beaten down by their overwhelming sensitivities. What is as heartbreaking for me today as it was in college is when an adult, particularly one in a white coat that holds a lot of authority, tells a young person how to define themselves by their pathology. When I co-hosted the Jedi Camp with an extraordinary yoga studio founder and teacher named Lisa Weber, a sixteen-year-old boy was in the camp. During introductions, he said, "I am a depressed and anxious teen." I was stunned.

"You're a what?" I asked again, without any grace or sensitivity.

Kevin repeated his statement, his head hung low.

"No, Kevin, you are not a 'depressed and anxious teen,'" I said, trying to hide my disgust that any teen would be prompted to say such words. "Who told you that you were?" I guessed that Kevin had not originated this description of himself.

"My psychiatrist," he said, as if he were declaring, "God said it."

"Well, your psychiatrist is wrong, Kevin," I said with conviction. "You are a brilliant spirit who is so sensitive that you pick up others' suffering and it makes you feel bad. It hurts, but that is a gift, not a pathology. When you say 'I am,' you are making an important declaration. It is OK to say that you are feeling sad or fearful when you are. That is different than declaring that you are your feelings or you are the feelings that medicine helps you not feel."

This was the first time Kevin made eye contact, and I saw hope there.

"When you are what you feel," I said to everyone in the class, "you are stuck and there is no way out. 'I am depressed' is simply untrue. 'I don't want to feel the pain of all that I'm feeling right now, so I choose to depress it for the time being' is an accurate statement.

"It is OK to say that. Just remember to be clear and truthful about it. And do not let anyone with authority tell you who you are or convince you that you are anything but a brilliant spirit on a human journey who may be, at the moment, experiencing painful challenges.

Do not give the power of your ever-hopeful spirit to a person who doesn't think there is any hope."

It was very hard for me to send prayers of love and peace to that psychiatrist, rather than wanting to throttle him or her for diminishing the esteem of a gifted young man. That person in the white coat had just given this young man drugs without giving him either hope or help. This psychiatrist, unlike the growing number I know who are holistically aware, cannot see Kevin's gift, name it, or help him better understand how to develop it and use it in service. It is the psychiatrist, in this case, who is limited and needs an expanded map of reality in order to help his patient.

After doing particular exercises to explore energy and sensitivity, Kevin found a few ways to think differently about himself and his gifts and to reclaim some of his power.

THE QUESTION RETURNS: PATHOLOGY OR GIFT?

Sometimes a parent calls because her child was diagnosed as learning disordered and she is not satisfied with the diagnosis. I am neither a medical practitioner nor a medical intuitive, who looks at the physical aspects of a person's energy and makes helpful suggestions, such as specific nutritional supplements.

Though I have had sixteen months of basic training in somatic psychotherapy, which often informs my perspective, I was never certified, and therefore I am not licensed to practice psychotherapy.

What I See is purely energetic and/or spiritual, and is typically related to behavioral and emotional patterns and essential gifts. In the next story, oddly, Paden's essential gifts were the reason for her diagnosis of "learning disordered."

When Camille called and asked me to Read her seven-year-old daughter, Paden, she said Paden had just been diagnosed with ADHD, and she simply didn't believe it. So I asked Camille to say her daughter's name. Then I Read something quite intriguing.

Paden's energy lit up with stories of lifetimes where she was tuned into the detail of fine arts in such a way that, as a male Chinese calligrapher, it took thirty years before her brush stroke was considered masterful. She was also revered for perfecting the art of the Japanese tea ceremony, where every small movement is considered important to the gift of the experience.

Now Paden goes to a traditional school. For her, it is as though someone took one teacup off the platter of the tea ceremony and said to her, "This cup is made in China. It's blue. It holds tea. Memorize that. It's important." This kind of education is an affront to her sensibilities. She is more refined and sensitive than that, more tuned into the whole.

I explained, "Paden can only learn when what she is learning has a bigger context. Steiner schools are one example of this kind of learning. When they learn about Russia, for example, they simultaneously learn about what Russians wear, eat, sing, dance, and export and about their language. Montessori is another school that provides holistic education.

Paden's mom told me that Paden was indeed very careful with her pen and seemed extraordinarily attuned to fine arts. Her physician wanted to prescribe medication, and her teachers had agreed. Thankfully, Paden's parents changed her school, and she is doing very well, without any medication.

Again, the list of behaviors on which Paden's doctors had based their diagnosis included not paying attention, inability to focus, and a wandering mind. Given Paden's gifts, the functional, mechanical way that education is offered could not be digested by her broader understanding of how to make meaning in the world. Her "symptoms" were simply her inability to be in alignment with a map of reality that was less complex than what she innately knew.

TOO MUCH INFORMATION

Sometimes my work allows me to observe how a child takes in stimuli from the environment and how he processes that data. In this case, a young man's medical diagnosis had an interesting correlation with what I energetically Saw. However, just as when I saw Liz's son's possession differently than the other Christian Seer, my perceptions indicated different treatment options. Here is the phone Reading. I have not to date met either the mother or the teen involved:

Angie called me about her sixteen-year-old son, Jason. "I don't know what to do with him. He is not doing well in school. Jason is so unhappy there. He is distracted, inattentive, and restless. He has always been sensitive, and I'm baffled as to how to help him." That is all Angie said about Jason.

As she said her son's full name, it was immediately clear to me that his mind was brilliant and his energy was highly dynamic and very busy. Then there was a feeling of great frustration and discomfort. I Saw a picture of a catfish being mistaken for a sardine and being the last one pushed into the can before sealing it.

Moving my lens out, I sought to understand how Jason was taking in and processing the energy around him. I Saw a broad dash of indigo color in the area of his third eye (energetically located between our two eyes), which was wide open. I witnessed how he would walk into a room and perceive the biofields or energy around people and objects. Although this was very natural for him, his "extra" sense caused him to feel continually overwhelmed.

It is not uncommon to see intuitively gifted children with their third eye wide open. To have foresight, insight, hindsight, and/or the ability to See horizontally into the future is the function of the third eye. When it is all the way open, the child is experiencing life holographically—the way I See energy in Readings. That means he may be able to Sense people's motivations and thoughts, and See the energy among different relationships, as well as Seeing colors and/or spirits. This is an overwhelming amount of data.

In addition, an open third eye means that the child is Seeing everything at once—without order or sequence—and everything is urgent. Thus there is a felt-need to quickly take care of everything simultaneously, with little ability to prioritize. These children see life as one busy, moving photograph. Then adults ask them to put the picture in sequenced order. There are no priorities or sequences in a photograph.

These children are often diagnosed with a learning disorder such as ADD—and told that this is because they cannot pay attention. As Mike, the principal from the boys' school in Canada said, "These children are paying far more attention than those who are labeling them as 'disordered' and 'inattentive.'" Without being given the tools to understand their intuitive gift and how to develop it, they are lost in a world whose map is too small to include their reality.

I asked Spirit to show me how Jason processed information, particularly information he sensed as emotionally threatening or overwhelming.

I Saw the energy from his perceptions flow together and enter his solar plexus, or rib cage area, with the force of water from a fire hydrant. The energy was entering his solar plexus because this is the area, according to the Hindu chakra system, where information about role and responsibility reside. Jason considered it his role to be a good student and his responsibility to understand and process everything that was occurring in the classroom.

Jason's coping mechanism immediately directed the energy to split, shooting it in two opposite directions—one energetic beam went to his head, where he tried to figure out what was happening, using his very high IQ, and the other went down to the base of his spine, his first chakra, where the information about what makes him feel safe and grounded resides. The assault of energy around Jason caused him to feel unsafe, and he was contracting around the base of his spine, holding onto his grounding for dear life.

One of the basic things I did to help Jason with his overwhelming feelings was to lower the "lid" on his third eye, and asked Angie to teach Jason the simple technique of becoming aware of his third eye (located in the middle of the forehead), to practice imagining that it was open all the way, halfway open, and then closed, and to experiment with how he felt in those different visualizations.

Typically, less data is noticed in the lower and closed positions, and this helps an intuitive feel less overwhelmed and more grounded. I also asked Angie to help Jason realize that he is neither crazy nor disordered, but that he has particular intuitive gifts that are meant to be developed and shared in service.

These gifts also come with the responsibility of maintaining the health of his exquisitely sensitive and balanced system. Young people with this gift do especially badly when they imbibe substances that alter brain chemistry.

It is important for them to ground through movement such as martial arts because these exercises teach them to keep their breath and energy in syncopation with their movement. In addition, I recommend a spiritual practice for these kids, so they can lift up or give what they perceive to Spirit, rather than assuming they need to take care of or fix what they intuitively perceive.

Here was the interesting part for me. After the Reading, Angie told me that Jason had been diagnosed as "bipolar" and was on medication for that. She shared that Jason had once remarked with great frustration: "Mom, when you walk into a room, you see tables and chairs. You can't possibly imagine everything I See around the tables and chairs—and the people!"

The bipolar diagnosis was an apt description of the energy's movement—a split from whole to two parts. However, because the physician could not see the energy and its path, the only way to serve Jason was to offer medication that prevents his frustration with the overwhelm by blocking his awareness. It does nothing to help him identify and learn about his gifts or how to manage them. Nor does it prepare him for the future.

REFLECTION

Intuitively and spiritually gifted children have been teaching me that they need a very specific kind of support—one that honors both them and their gifts. As I continue to meet with parents and children, I am convinced there is an imperative to define intuitive developmental pathways.

Then, just as kids who are outstanding in math might get advanced work in that area, children with intuitive gifts can access higher-level understanding of the dynamics of energy, spirit, and intuition.

I see hope and relief in the eyes of the kids who come to me, when they hear that there are role models who are contributing their intuitive gifts to make a positive difference in the world.

From the summer I spent with the kids in Jedi Camp, I learned that all the children—perhaps all human beings—benefit from the following:
- knowing how to build healthy boundaries
- learning about and staying grounded in present time
- finding their center and knowing how to manage power
- building a loyal relationship with the God of their hearts and evolving their spiritual practice

CHAPTER FOURTEEN

Mainstreaming Intuitive Intelligence

Having devoted some of my work to Reading, researching, and working in the area of children with intuitive gifts, this is my current perspective:

Perceiving invisible realms is a function and application of intuitive intelligence—in whatever form it takes. By paying attention to our intuitive capacities, we are reclaiming a natural brain function that has not been advanced or developed as other intelligences have because we are largely afraid of it, and have sensationalized or demonized its utility. In embracing and developing the intuitive brain function, we also, then, have greater capacity to partner with the invisible realms.

This brain capacity offers us the opportunity to understand that our invisible map of reality has the power to influence our lives in significant ways. It is the portal to greater meaning and purpose in our lives. Each of us is born with intuitive intelligence, and we can cultivate its potential to the degree we choose.

It is becoming more prominent in an increasing number of hypersensitive children. This is precisely because the future depends upon our ability to partner intuitive intelligence with rational intelligence (as well as other intelligences) to devise quick and comprehensive solutions to address complex, interrelated global challenges. Intuitive intelligence can bring data to the table in a way, a time frame, and often with a kind of accuracy that logic and analysis simply cannot.

The way I know the work I do is part of intuitive intelligence is this: I often only know my client's name and the challenge he articulates. I close my eyes, and from my third eye, I Read my client's energy field. For one and a half hours, I tell story after story, from what role the client was playing to what happened from the perspective of the client's role, to what he was thinking and feeling, to how he made meaning of what happened, to what he came to believe about himself and the situation, to what fear-based belief he decided to create—which forms the underpinning of his current challenge.

I identify the fear that sits beneath all the stories related to his challenge. Releasing that fear and related beliefs, we replace them with life-giving beliefs through visualization.

These stories are completely nonsensical to anyone else listening and often even to me, since I know nothing about the client before he walks in or calls me for a Reading.

Then something truly extraordinary happens.

At the end of the Reading, I open my eyes, and 99 percent of the time the person is nodding slowly, saying, "Yes, that makes sense. I see. Yes, that makes perfect sense."

That is the most astounding part of my work. I Read stories that the analytical mind could not possibly imagine as being logically related to the challenges at hand. The logical mind must step aside, as intuition does its magic in holographically locating through stories and symbols a more robust understanding of the challenge.

As the intuitive mind completes its circuitous motion, identifying specific images and voices that emerge from a client's hidden map, the logical mind steps back in to examine the data there assembled. The logical mind provides an enabling structure that sorts the data into a sequence it can understand, and then the two parts come together as the logical mind accepts the intuitive intelligence as valid: "Yes, it all makes perfect sense."

If we are to prepare our children for the world and our world for the future, it is critical to begin to understand intuitive intelligence, which can access the unconscious beliefs and motives that fuel human dynamics.

In my next book, named after my Chicagonow.com blog, *From Paranormal to Pretty Normal: Intuition at the Center,* I will delve more deeply into the stories of what I have Seen in the intuitive realms about children and teens, what they are here to teach us, and how we can be a blessing and support for their development in ways that balance their unique needs. My DVDs on Intuitive Intelligence offer a curriculum for understanding, sorting, and developing particular kinds of intuitive intelligence because I believe everyone benefits when befriending this brain function and soul-level gift.

I hope my journey has further opened, with compassionate understanding, your invisible map of reality. I hope you will embrace your intuitive intelligence—which is native to both our species and native to your uniqueness—and begin to develop it. If we were all to do that, what a world we could know!

Conclusion: *Imagining the Future*

Mapping a New Reality can take us to a point where Earth is very different because of our choices. Here is one version of what is possible:

Imagine that, instead of regular spiritual practice to keep us in touch with Spirit, it is our most natural state to know we are Light beings, fully and completely part of Spirit.

Moments of humanity occur when something feels different from our usual joy. Right then and there, our instinct is to immediately send compassion to whomever or whatever is impacted.

At the same time, we create a loving boundary around human moments to support those involved without judgment, and honor whatever happens as learning. Then we thank those involved for reminding us of the wisdom inherent in all moments, including this one. We stand together and allow each being to learn as it chooses, knowing that soon each difference will be returned to the realization that our most natural identity is as beloved beings of Light.

IMAGINE...

Imagine, as John Lennon suggested, that violence, greed, jealousy, hatred, and materialism are so foreign to our nature that we simply find them uninteresting qualities, therefore having no desire to create anything that contains these elements.

Imagine that human curiosity is the fuel for positive, complementary, and collaborative creation that occurs in as many ways as our creativity can take us.

Imagine that our greatest desire and joy is to find out about others—their ideas and gifts and what they care about.

Imagine looking with loving attention toward others to understand how they want to employ their imagination. Imagine that we want to relate to them or help them connect to ways or others who would add to their fun and joy.

Imagine that everyone is clear that our existence is eternal, and that we very naturally make the best and most of every moment now.

We have the collective capacity to create this world...and maybe this is scheduled for our next epoch.

Maybe it is what the intuitively and spiritually gifted children are here to teach us.

Why not claim it now and accelerate the creation of this new map of reality?

BIBLIOGRAPHY

These resources have informed and inspired me on the path referenced in *Mapping a New Reality*. I trust you will explore other works by the same authors if you find these references helpful and inspiring!

Alli, Antero. *Angel Tech: A Modern Shaman's Guide to Reality Selection.* New Falcon Publications: Santa Monica, California, 1994.

Argüelles, José, and Charles Tart. *Earth Ascending: An Illustrated Treatise on Law Governing Whole Systems.* Bear and Company: Santa Fe, New Mexico, 1988.

Armstrong, Karen. *A History of God: The 4,000-Year Quest of Judaism, Christianity, and Islam.* Ballantine Books: New York, 1993.

Beevers, John. *The Autobiography of Saint Therese of Lisieux: The Story of a Soul.* Double Day: New York, 2006.

Branden, Gregg. *The Isaiah Effect: Decoding the Lost Science of Prayer and Prophecy.* Three Rivers Press: New York, 2000.

Brinkley, Dannion. *Saved by the Light: The True Story of a Man Who Died Twice and the Profound Revelations He Received.* Harper Collins Books: New York, 2008.

Brown, Courtney. *Cosmic Voyage: A Scientific Discovery of Extraterrestrials Visiting Earth.* Hodder & Stoughton: New York, 1997.

Chadha, Yogesh. *Gandhi: A Life.* Century Books: United Kingdom, 1997.

Cooperrider, David L., and Diana Whitney. *Appreciative Inquiry: A Positive Revolution in Change.* Barrett-Kohler: San Francisco, 2005.

Deal, Terry and Allan Kennedy, *Corporate Cultures: The Rites and Rituals of Corporate Life.* Perseus Books Publishing, LLC: San Francisco, 2000.

Eckhart, Meister, and Oliver Davies. *Selected Writings.* Penguin Classics: London, 1995.

Ferguson, Marilyn. *The Aquarian Conspiracy: Personal and Social Transformation in the 1980s.* Tarcher Books: New York, 1980.

Grendlin, Eugene, PhD. *Focusing*. Bantum Dell: New York, 2007.

Judith, Anodea. *Wheels of Life: A User's Guide to the Chakra System*. Llewellyn's New Age Series: Woodbury, Minnesota, 2006.

Kubler-Ross, Elizabeth, MD. *On Death and Dying*. Tavistock Publications Unlimited: Great Britian, 1970.

Kurtz, Ron, PhD. *Hakomi Body-Centered Psychotherapy: The Hakomi Method: The Integrated Use of Mindfulness, Nonviolence, and the Body*. Liferhythm Publishers: Mendocino, California, 1997.

MacLaine, Shirley. *Out on a Limb*. Bantum Books: New York, 1984.

Masters, Robert. *Neurospeak: Transforms Your Body as You Read*. Quest Books: Illinois, 1994.

Owen, Harrison. *Open Space Technology: A User's Guide*. Barrett-Kohler: San Francisco, 2008.

Robinson, Sir Ken. *RSA Animate: Changing Education Paradigms*. YouTube. www.youtube.com/watch?v=zDZFcDGpL4U.

Rowley, Therese, PhD. "The Multi-sensory Child." *Children of the New Earth* (2005). http://www.childrenofthenewearth.com/features.php?page=articles/rowley_therese/article1.

Satir, Virginia. *The New Peoplemaking*. Science and Behavior Books: Palo Alto, California, 1988.

Scott, Cynthia, and Dennis Jaffe. *Managing Change at Work: Leading People through Organizational Transitions*. A Crisp Publication: San Francisco, 1989.

Teresa of Avila, and David Lewis. *Life of St. Teresa of Jesus*. The Echo Library: Middlesex, Twickenham, 2006.

Tucker, James, M.D. *Life Before Life: Children's Memories of Previous Lives*. St. Martin Press: New York, 2005.

ABOUT THE AUTHOR

Therese Rowley, Ph.D., has been a strategic change management consultant for more than 25 years. She weaves her understanding of intuitive intelligence with her corporate experience to facilitate large scale business transformation in industries such as telecommunications, manufacturing, market research and financial services.

Therese counsels business leaders seeking to align their personal and business missions. She speaks professionally on the topics of leadership, transformation and using intuitive intelligence for both professional and personal success. Therese founded the Conscious Business Network to explore the new capitalism and reach out to businesses and professionals committed to fostering integrity and transparency in the marketplace.

Therese Rowley has performed thousands of Intuitive Readings for those on a spiritual or conscious path as well as for parents of intuitively gifted children whom she finds are often misdiagnosed with learning disorders.

The author holds a Ph.D. in Organizational Transformation from Union Institute and University, an MBA from Northwestern University Kellogg School of Management and a Masters in Public Administration from the University of Denver. She has also done extended study in somatic psychotherapy and over 50 different healing modalities.

Therese Rowley writes a blog for ChicagoNow.com, a Tribune company blog network, called "From Paranormal to Pretty Normal, Intuition at the Center" and one for The Huffington Post called "Inner Wisdom". Her media interviews include Dr. Mehmet Oz, Chicago's NBC and ABC affiliates, and WLS and WGN Radio.